Castlevania
— Lords of Shadow —
Official Strategy Guide

Characters 4

Bestiary 9

Items 22

Skills 26

Basic Actions 26

Advanced Moves 28

Secondary Weapons 30

Mounts 31

Relic Powers 32

Relic Moves List 32

Walkthrough 39

Chapter One 40

Besieged Village 40

Hunting Path 44

The Dead Bog 47

Pan's Temple 54

Oblivion Lake 58

Chapter Two 62

Enchanted Forest 62

Underground Caves 68

Labyrinth Entrance 73

Waterfalls of Agharta 78

Agharta 84

Dark Dungeon 88

Sanctuary Entrance 93

Sanctuary of Titans 98

The Black Knight 102

Chapter Three 104

The Three Towers 104

The Dark Lord of the Lycanthropes 114

Chapter Four 118

Mountain Fortress 118

The Crow Witch 127

Chapter Five — 134

Veros Woods — 134

Wygol Village — 138

Abbey Catacombs — 142

Abbey Library — 147

Abbey Tower — 152

Brauner — 155

Castle Sewers — 158

Chapter Six — 161

Castle Courtyard — 161

Maze Gardens — 165

Castle Hall — 169

Refectory — 173

Chapter Seven — 178

Balcony — 178

Electric Laboratory — 182

Chromatic Observatory — 186

Chapter Eight — 191

Outer Wall — 191

The Clockwork Tower — 195

Olrox — 199

The Throne Room — 202

Chapter Nine — 206

Bones Forest — 206

Woes Moor — 211

The Music Box — 214

Chapter Ten — 218

Titan Graveyard — 218

Fire Pinnacle — 224

Fire Cemetery — 227

Crematory Oven — 232

Chapter Eleven — 236

Necromancer's Abyss — 236

The Dracolich — 245

Chapter Twelve — 249

Final Fight — 249

Achievements/Trophies — 252

Extras — 254

CHARACTERS

MAIN CHARACTERS

Gabriel

As an infant he was found abandoned at the door of one of the Brotherhood of Light convents. It is not known who his original parents were. Some suspect that he was the unwanted bastard of a wealthy landowner, most likely from the Cronqvist family, though this has never been proved. The Order named the boy after the blessed Archangel Gabriel and raised him as one of its own. A precocious child, he quickly proved to be extremely talented, developing an unprecedented mastery of the fighting arts. Gabriel took the surname of Belmont from his love of the mountains and the high places of the world.

Prone to dark moods and occasional ambivalence, Gabriel was deeply affected by the death of his childhood sweetheart, Marie. He has embarked on this quest at the request of the elders of the Brotherhood, and has a burning desire for revenge.

Marie

Marie, the youngest daughter of a rich merchant family, was always attracted by the courageous nature of the Brotherhood of the Light; curious and lively, she often escaped her duties at home in order to help the monks, baking and cleaning for them. During one of these visits she became acquainted with the boy that would later become her husband, an orphan by the name of Gabriel.

The two youngsters were made for each other; they grew up together and made promises for the future. These promises were kept when, one idyllic morning, with the blessing of both her family and the Brotherhood, the couple were married. Marie provided a good counterpoint to Gabriel's dark moods, and often just her laughter was enough to blow away the gathering storm within him.

Now Marie has been tragically murdered and Gabriel seeks revenge.

Pan

Classic folklore tells of a mystical spirit that inhabits untamed woodlands, protecting them from harm. Legends tell of different forms to this spirit: an eagle, a deer, a boar, or even a horse. Some portray Pan as an evil satyr, while others tell a story of a benevolent and powerful demi-god, servant of Mother Nature herself. But Mankind, in its arrogance, pollutes and destroys the world, and the old spirits depart—and soon Pan must choose his own fate.

Zobek

If the chronicles of the Brotherhood are to be believed, Zobek is one of their longest serving warriors. The list of heroic deeds attributed to him is as impressive as his vast knowledge of the art of war. Despite his age, he can deploy mighty fighting skills. His weapon of choice is a simple long sword, which he handles with great skill. Usually, he likes to wear the old-fashioned uniform of the Brotherhood of Light that, according to him, was inherited from one of his ancestors, one of the founding members of the Order.

Claudia

Claudia is a mute orphan girl who lives in the ruins of Agharta, the destroyed capital of a once-great civilization. The race that created the city lived very long lives, often over many centuries, and Claudia shares this trait. Having endured innumerable years in the dust and decay, she has developed telepathic powers by communicating with her loyal guardian, the Black Knight. This is an ancient form of communication favored by her ancestors. The strong bond that she has developed with her armored protector has saved them both on many occasions. Claudia is brave and carefree, unafraid to confront danger. Yet deep within is a sadness that will never leave her, the loss of her beloved father.

Vincent Dorin

The abbey at Wygol had always been a place of peace and meditation. The monks that inhabited it were considered great scribes, and their wonderfully crafted manuscripts made the abbey a destination for holy pilgrimage. The current abbot, Father Dorin, was an erudite scholar, devoted to the study of the old texts retained in the abbey's vast library. Shutting himself away, he studied these ancient texts and prophetic scrolls for years, turning half blind and quite mad in the process. When the Vampires came, he discovered a holy relic hidden deep in the library that kept the evil creatures at bay. In order to preserve the holy books and himself, he banished everyone from the abbey and disassociated himself from his people, leaving them to their fate without protection.

Laura

The child-like appearance of Laura has led many to their deaths, for she is a deceptive, ruthless killer who has murdered hundreds of innocents over many centuries to satiate her blood craving. Although she has the body of a child, she has the cunning and intellect of someone far older. She can be particularly cruel, often treating the killing of her victims as a game. However, when at rest and alone, she remembers a time long past, a time of warmth and comfort and a woman's beautiful voice singing to her as she sleeps, comforting her in the darkness—a life lost long ago.

Baba Yaga

This old hag is the subject of many a myth in popular folklore, mostly appearing as an evil witch who eats children and lives in a cabin that stands on a pair of chicken legs. While parts of these legends are true, her house does not stand on chicken legs, though as for the rest—who knows? Baba Yaga likes to brew a special tea made from extremely rare blue rose petals, which temporarily transforms this hideous old hag into a beautiful young woman. Although she sometimes helps people, it's usually very dangerous to ask her for a favor, unless you are very polite and can offer her something in return.

Lord of the Dead

Lord of all the Dead, he is death personified and with his knowledge of the dark arts none may stand against him, living or dead.

Bestiary

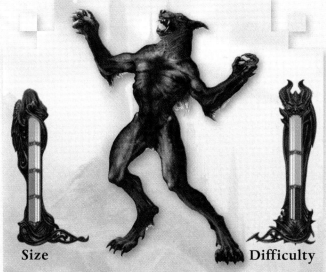

Size   Difficulty

Lesser Lycanthrope

These creatures are humans that have been poisoned with an infectious disease known as the "Werewolf Influenza," which is transmitted, in most cases, by the bite of another Lycanthrope. There is an old saying that goes like this, "If you are bitten by a Lycan, better to let it gnaw," and like most proverbs, it is more true than not. Once infected with the disease, the transformation process can be completed in only a few minutes.

Size   Difficulty

Greater Lycanthrope

Greater or "pureblood" Lycanthropes are those spawned from the Dark Lord himself. In these cases, their condition is not considered a disease, as the transformation process has been deliberately chosen. The endowment of lycanthropy, however, is not given to just anyone by the Dark Lord, and only a handful of his more loyal acolytes have received such a gift. The Dark Lord keeps these elite guards for special missions, and they are not only fearsome but also incredibly intelligent and formidable foes in combat.

Size   Difficulty

Warg

Little is known about these fierce, wolf-like beasts, except that they appeared soon after the coming of the Lycanthrope Dark Lord. Despite their wild looks, Wargs are fairly intelligent creatures, capable of being tamed by lesser Lycanthopes, who ride them in battle. Wargs are ferocious creatures that attack opponents with razor-sharp claws and sharp, deadly teeth.

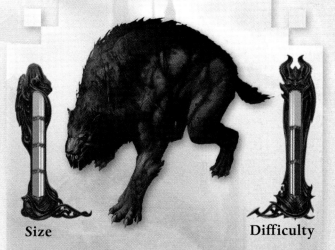

Size   Difficulty

Great Warg

Wargs are the principal strength of large Lycanthrope raiding parties. Some of them are "blessed" by the Dark Lord himself which gives them new powers, such as improved strength and wound regeneration. Due to the nature of the "blessing," these powers are heightened by a full moon.

Goblin

These diminutive, mischievous and crabby creatures usually avoid contact with humans. Goblins make their homes around tree roots and mossy damp areas, and like to hunt in packs. Although they can be aggressive when threatened, Goblins usually prefer to keep far from men and their dwellings. Goblins are a species on the verge of extinction, and before too long will pass into history and then myth.

Size   Difficulty

Naiad

A large part of the danger in the swamps lies in the hands of creatures known as Naiads. These living things are usually passive, lying inconspicuously on riverbeds and muddy, damp places, waiting until someone stumbles within range. When they attack, their unfortunate victims usually mistake their limbs for branches and are soon drowned—and eaten. In days gone by, these beautiful creatures were worshipped and sacrifices were made to them, but they are now forgotten by humans and have become evil predators, plaguing both wandering man and beast alike.

Size   Difficulty

Size   Difficulty

Swamp Troll

Swamp trolls are a rare subspecies of the larger Cave Troll. Although similar in appearance to their dry land cousins, the thick fur has been replaced with a slimy coating, similar to wet mould, which better suits the damper weather of their habitat. Swamp Trolls are ferocious in battle and display a cunning that belies their outward appearance.

Small Troll

Biologically speaking, small and great Trolls are more or less equal. However, their behavior couldn't be more different; the large subspecies is fairly aggressive, whereas Small Trolls are cowardly and quickly flee when outnumbered.

Size   Difficulty

Size   **Difficulty**

Cave Troll

Trolls are a dying species living mostly in mountainous areas. They are aggressive and territorial. This can sometimes result in attacks on humans who are foolish enough to encroach on the Troll's natural habitat. However, Cave Trolls are usually passive around their own kind and rarely attack each other. Men say that when Trolls die of old age they turn into stone and this can be clearly seen in certain rock formations if one looks closely enough.

Size   **Difficulty**

Ice Titan

Buried deep below the surface of an ancient lake, waiting to be found, are the remnants of a once great civilization. Before Rome, before ancient Greece, this great empire possessed technology that surpassed all others, and this Titan marks the pinnacle of their achievements. A great conflict known as "The Necromantic Wars" obliterated this once thriving civilization and this great feat of engineering was lost.

When the dark spell that isolated the heavens from our earthy plane was cast, the souls of the dead were drawn to this place and somehow gave new energy to the magic runes, reanimating the Titan one final time—

Giant Spider

These monsters are the largest type of known arachnids, and they are much more aggressive than any of the normal-sized varieties of Spider. Giant Spiders can be found in almost any environment, but they usually prefer dark, soggy places, such as old forests or grottos. Like their smaller counterparts, Giant Spiders can weave webs of sticky silk that they use to trap their prey before eating them. In fact, spider silk is extremely strong and can even be used to make rope of incredible durability. The Giant Spider population has shrunk in recent years due to human encroachment.

Size   **Difficulty**

Size   Difficulty

Warthog

The genealogy of these monstrous boars has been kept secret among Goblin tribes for centuries. It is a process that involves special breeding, feeding, and shaman magic. Warthogs are so scarce that having more than one of these mounts is something only a few Goblin tribes can aspire to. Goblins not only use them for riding into battle but also to consume all the rubbish and leftover scraps of food, thus helping to maintain a clean environment.

Size   Difficulty

Gremlin

Gremlins are small, winged imps, famous for causing havoc wherever they go. Gremlins travel in large groups, infesting buildings until the occupants either escape in fear or die. Gremlins are able to breathe fire, an ability inherited from their demon ancestors, but their small bodies cannot withstand too much punishment. They are very volatile and tend to explode if hit hard enough.

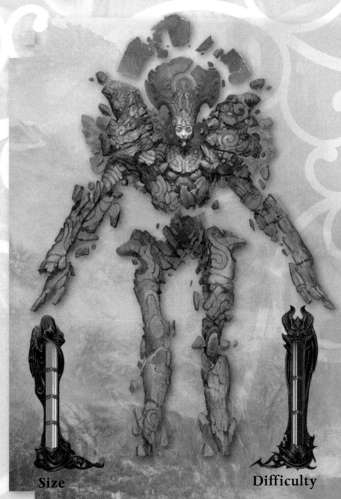

Size   Difficulty

Stone Idol Titan

The Mage-Smiths were an order of Aghartian wizards who specialized in the creation of powerful artifacts. Most of their inventions were objects of common use, such as magical clothing or enchanted weapons and armor, but probably their most impressive creations were the Titans. These golems of gargantuan proportions were built for defensive purposes, but mages were forced to use them in the course of the war against the Dark Lords, during which most of them were destroyed.

Size  Difficulty

Black Knight Golem

This Golem was created using similar techniques to those involved in the construction of the Titans. However, a human body was needed to imbue the armor with great power, so Claudia's father used the corpse of a mute killer and weaved his soul within the armor to forge this magical being. The Black Knight requires souls in order to function, so Claudia lures evil creatures so that he may devour them. Despite this, the Black Knight is not evil; the soul of the killer inside the armor hopes for redemption by protecting his ward, and sees a kindred spirit in the mute daughter of his creator, whom he has eventually grown to love.

Size 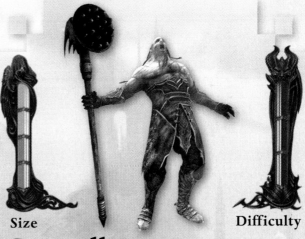 Difficulty

Cornell

The three founding members of the Brotherhood of Light were brave warriors who sacrificed their physical bodies in order to become spiritual beings, able to fight God's wars against evil. They performed a mystical ritual to transform themselves into angelic creatures. Their intentions were honorable, but they were deceived and their spirits were fractured; their good sides were transported to Heaven as angelic beings, while their dark sides were left behind. Cornell was the youngest of the three, but he was also the strongest. Unlike his companions, he rarely used his magic powers, preferring to fight using a great sledgehammer that none but he could wield. On that fateful night, the spirit of Cornell left his body, and all the strength and anger left behind gave birth to the Lycanthrope Dark lord.

Lycanthrope Dark Lord

The Dark Lord of the Lycanthropes is the personification of hate and violence. In his werewolf form he has superhuman strength and speed, far greater than even his mighty lieutenants.

In addition to his natural abilities, he can also use the power of the Cyclone Boots: magical relics worn by his human counterpart. With them, he is able to jump great distances and perform powerful charge movements that can tear down most obstacles.

Size Difficulty

Ogre

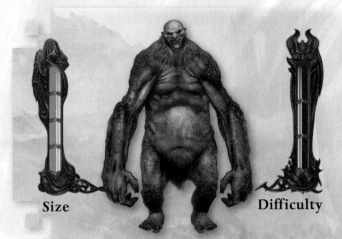

Size

Difficulty

The Anubian Giants are an ancient species, as old as the Earth itself. This particular Ogre is one of the last of his race left in the world. He lives amongst the walls of this deserted mountain fortress, waiting for misguided travelers to stumble in, so that he can grind their bones to make his bread. However, this particular Ogre hasn't had much man flesh for quite some time, having to settle for the odd cave troll. Ogres have an extremely keen sense of smell and can sniff a man from half-a-mile away, making them very successful trackers. Fortunately their size and clumsy nature means that their prey can often see or hear them coming!

Chupacabras

Often portrayed as evil, blood-sucking monsters, the Chupacabras only real obsessions are magical relics. When in the presence of such artifacts, they do anything to get them. However, the Chupacabras are not inherently evil creatures, and most of the time, after a short game of hide and seek, will return anything they have stolen.

Size

Difficulty

Swordmaster

Size

Difficulty

"The spirit of a brave fighter never dies," according to a popular saying and, in some places filled with the foul magic energy, the soul of a slain warrior doesn't leave the material plane but remains trapped. These restless souls usually cover themselves in ragged clothes, maybe as a remnant of their living past. Apart from their fighting skills, they have lost all vestiges of humanity.

Crow Witch Malphas

It is said that this monster was once a beautiful woman, a Witch who inhabited the mountains that surrounded the fortress. During this time she fell in love with a Prince who lived in the Keep. Besotted with him, she used her powers to concoct potions of love and enchantment so that she could have him for herself. Alas, another Witch entrapped him and he met a most gruesome end. Mad with grief, Malphas threw herself from the top of the tower and landed on the rocks below. Incredibly, she survived the fall, though her body was horribly broken. The crows fed on her and she on them. Her cries of maddened rage fill the long, dark valleys below the fortress and echo around the tower that was once a place of love and hope.

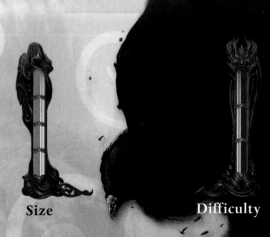

Size

Difficulty

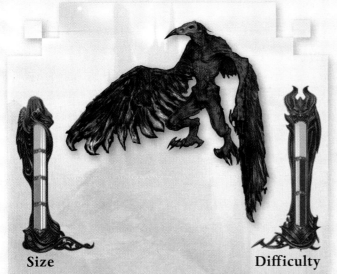

Size   Difficulty

Witch Child

These half human, half bird-like creatures are the progeny of the Crow Witch, Malphas. The Witch-children are able to breathe fire and are extremely volatile, oftentimes dying in a blazing explosion. However, like most magically summoned entities, their existence is short-lived and they tend to die naturally a few days after their "birth."

Size   Difficulty

Ghoul

Despite most people believing otherwise, Ghouls are not undead creatures. In fact, their ancestors were human, but a diet of corpses and rotten flesh transformed them into horrible monsters that dwell in burial grounds and cemeteries. Ghouls usually live underground, but sometimes venture outside in small groups to scavenge for carrion. The vomit of the Ghoul is highly poisonous, but can be dispelled using Light Magic.

Size   Difficulty

Vampire Warrior

A Vampire can be born from different creatures; the ceremony itself involves the exchange of blood between the "host" and the soon-to-be Vampire. However, vampirism has to be accepted by the recipient, so it remains exclusive to intelligent creatures. The lowest ranked Vampires usually take the form of a creature with a bat-like appearance. Over the centuries, as they become more powerful, Vampires appear more human-like and are able to transform at will from hideous creatures into human form. One can usually ascertain the power of a Vampire by its appearance and any Vampires that appear totally human are usually incredibly powerful and extremely dangerous. These particular Vampire Warriors show the signs of being recently turned.

Animated Armor

These empty suits of armor have been given a temporary "life" due to the possession by a poltergeist. They serve the Vampire Dark Lord by patrolling and protecting the castle's halls and corridors. The spirit of this poltergeist can move from armor to armor if it so wishes, though it can take many days for the spirit to recover when doing so. Once established within a suit of armor, the poltergeist can travel between dimensions at will, causing a huge electrical outage that signals an opening between our world and the spirit world. You can tell when armor is possessed because a strange unearthly, reddish glow emanates from within the suit, indicating that its ghostly inhabitant is awake.

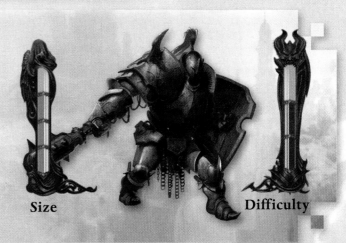

Size   Difficulty

Lieutenant Brauner

This Vampire is a powerful demon, turned by the Dark Lord long ago. It is well known that young Vampires are bestial in appearance, but as they become stronger, they are able to regain human form. Indeed, many of the oldest Vampires are mistaken for high-born aristocracy. However, this creature was never human and thus cannot take that form. Rather, he is a spawn of hell, possessing vampiric powers, which make him a formidable foe.

Size   Difficulty

Commander Olrox

Another demon-spawned Vampire, he and his younger sibling were both inhuman before the Dark Lord found them and turned them. In fact, they didn't belong to this earthly plane at all, being lesser nether demons begat in the deepest corners of Hell. How they came into our world is still a mystery, but what is known is that the Vampire Dark Lord found them and used her influence upon them.

Size   Difficulty

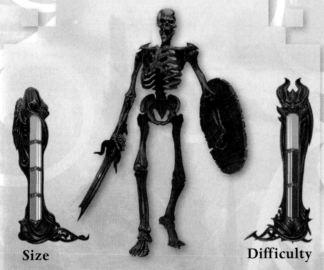

Size   Difficulty

Skeleton Warrior

The human inhabitants of the Vampire Castle suffered a cruel fate. While most of them changed into Vampire Warriors, a few, mainly those who were the Dark Lord's most loyal retainers when she was human, were made into Skeleton Warriors by the spell of the Puppeteer.

Unlike other beings animated by this magic, the vestiges of a once human soul make Skeleton Warriors difficult to command and are therefore rarely found in groups greater that two or three.

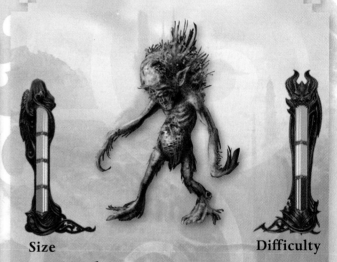

Size   Difficulty

Mandragora

Common ingredients in the creation of magic potions, Mandrake Roots are an important resource for alchemists and mages the world over. However, the harvesting of Mandrake Roots is a dangerous activity; when the root is dug up, the plant will scream loudly, killing anyone near it. When they are fully grown, Mandrakes become Mandragora, sentient beings who survive by draining the life force of nearby creatures.

Evil Butcher

This monster of unknown origin has somehow become the "official cook" for the Vampires. The Dark Lord uses the Evil Butcher to feed the Ghouls, Wargs, and other creatures that live within the castle grounds.

He carries a huge iron cleaver. He is not really a fighter, but is dangerous and skilled with the tools found in his kitchen. He needs constant "refueling" in order to maintain his stamina.

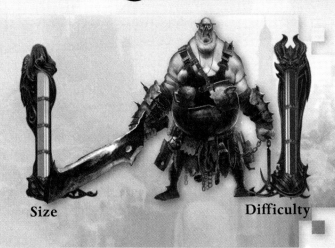

Size   **Difficulty**

Size   **Difficulty**

Mechanical Monstrosity

The Vampires were not the first tenants of the castle; the previous owner was a scientist known as Friedrich Von Frankenstein. He used the caste to conceal his horrific experiments into artificial life. The Mechanical Monstrosity was one such foray. Frankenstein created this giant scorpion-like machine using the brain of a malformed medical experiment gone wrong. However, his creature proved difficult to control and now rampages through the castle killing anything it can get its claws into.

Deadly Toys

Laura, the "daughter" of the Vampire Lord, has brought these puppets into existence using a dark spell of her own making. She is able to control these toys and transfer the temporary life force from toy to toy, thus making them very difficult to defeat. However, so long as the "spirit" within is defeated, they cannot return. Inside the crude stitching is the source of the spell and, by opening up the deadly toys, one can destroy the spell.

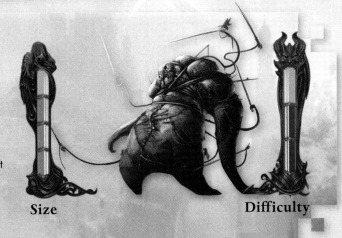

Size   **Difficulty**

Size   **Difficulty**

Carmilla

The three founding members of the Brotherhood of Light were brave warriors who sacrificed their physical bodies in order to become spiritual beings, able to fight God's wars against evil. They performed a mystical ritual to transform themselves into angelic creatures. Their intentions were honorable, but they were deceived and their spirits were fractured; their good sides were transported to Heaven as angelic beings, while their dark sides were left behind. The second of the founders, Carmilla, was a highly skilled healer, and her talents knew no equal.

When the Spirit left her body on that fateful night, her love for life and her purity were corrupted, giving birth to the Vampire Dark Lord.

Vampire Dark Lord

Just like the Lycanthrope Dark Lord, the Vampire Queen was granted an animal-like manifestation of the dark parts of her spirit. It is pitifully ironic that for a healer with such a love for life, she would be transformed into a blood-sucking monster that consumes the energy of living creatures in order to survive. This ungodly bat demon uses the Seraph Shoulders to fly and can conjure up Vampire Warriors at will from anywhere in the castle to do her bidding.

Size

Difficulty

Headless Burrower

These undead creatures are the decapitated remains of warriors from the Brotherhood, Necromancer magic has reanimated them and they prey on fellow warriors who bear arms for the Brotherhood. Using their heads, they can attack at will biting and tearing their victims. However, it is their bodies that are their weak spot and anyone caught in a battle with Zombie Heads would do well to remember that!

Size

Difficulty

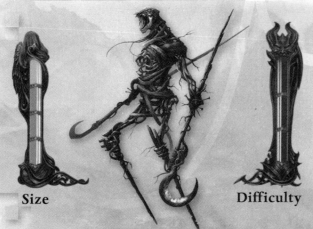

Size

Difficulty

Scarecrow

The Scarecrows are magical constructs of the Crow Witch Malphas that attack and kill anything that moves. Malphas created the Scarecrows to keep Baba Yaga under her watchful eye and, where possible, to nullify her power by restricting her movements. The Scarecrows are roused by the birds, which follow the evil Crow Witch's bidding. The scarecrows are extremely fast and attack with razor-sharp scythes.

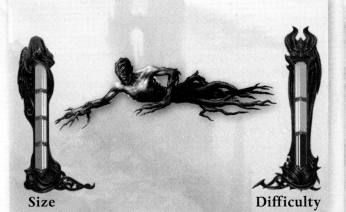

Size **Difficulty**

Creeping Corpse

There is a strange, magical root that only grows in the land of the dead, which feeds on the carcasses of the dead creatures. This plant consumes all of the organic material around it and, after it is satisfied, evolves from the corpses it has ingested to become a living being. Once fully grown, the creeping corpse looks for living creatures to devour.

Size **Difficulty**

Creeping Coffin

Sometimes, a Creeping Corpse feeds directly from a dead body still in its coffin; in such cases, the plant doesn't leave but instead uses the coffin as armor. For mobility, the creature plunges its branches through the sides of the coffin and extends them, becoming a four-legged monster that's even more dangerous than usual.

Size **Difficulty**

The Silver Warrior

Pan, once revered as a God, rarely changes into this form, preferring peace to protect all living things. The magical silver armor is a remnant of ancient times, a tool used for fighting the forces of evil. It hasn't been worn for centuries. Now, out of necessity, Pan adorns his body in this ancient armor to test Gabriel one final time. Pan puts his trust in God, for no knight that is false can survive the test of arms. The loser provides the ultimate sacrifice, according to God's will.

Zombie

Zombies are the most basic creations of a master Necromancer and form the rank and file of the Lord of the Dead's army. These reanimated corpses are an amalgam of different body parts, sewn together in a rough humanoid shape, so it is not uncommon to see Zombies with more than one head or multiple arms. Zombie carcasses are very fragile and weak, so they usually attack in large groups, using their numbers to overwhelm an enemy.

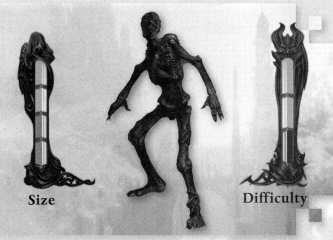

Size **Difficulty**

Gravedigger

The Necromancers had to keep a constant supply of corpses in order to build their army of the undead. To sustain the immense cemeteries where all these bodies were kept, the Necromancers relied on the Gravedigger, an enslaved, nameless demon mutated and empowered with the tainted magic of these evil sorcerers. The Gravedigger uses a giant shovel to exhume the dead, and this also makes a formidable weapon in combat.

Size **Difficulty**

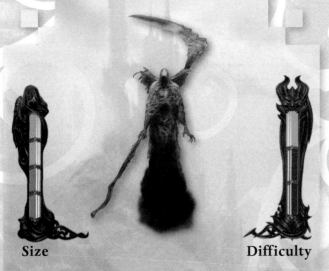

Size **Difficulty**

Reaper

Only powerful sorcerers can summon and control these dangerous spirits. The Reapers are a corporeal manifestation of Death itself; their aspect depends on the beliefs of those who confront them, but most people perceive the Reapers as skeletal figures with long tunics, wielding large scythes.

Size **Difficulty**

Necromancer

Necromancy is the most evil of all the schools of magic and can only be performed by the followers of the Dark Lord of the Dead. Unlike vampirism and lycanthropy, the powers necessary to control the energies of the deceased are not easily acquired. The Dark Lord only shares a small part of his power with his followers, who themselves must die in order to use the abilities given to them. Once dead, they become his thralls and their master is able to control them with his own considerable power.

Dracolich Titan

Necromancers are evil wizards who can control the dead with dark powers. The most common belief is that this power is limited to deceased humans but, in fact, it encompasses all dead creatures, as demonstrated by this monster, the reanimated carcass of a Dragon. This massive creature, a remnant of our pre-historic past, died long before the Necromancers came to this land and was buried under tons of rock, eventually becoming fossil.

When the Dark Lord built his fortress in this desolate land, he discovered the carcass and reconstructed it using magical runes to bind evil spirits to the ancient bones. Should the necessity arise, this monster is able to perform one last duty for its master.

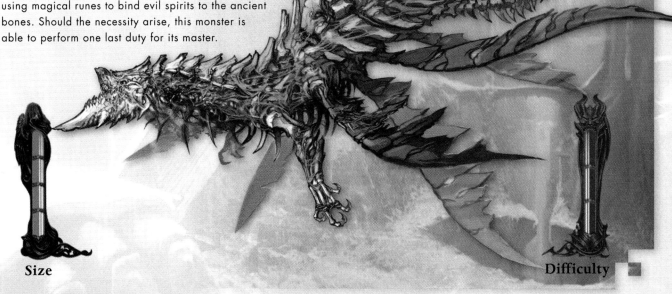

Size

Difficulty

Satan

The real mastermind behind these events, the fallen angel Satan was cast down to Earth as punishment for his rebellion against God. Satan has been searching for a way to re-enter Heaven and crush the Almighty once and for all. The God Mask is said to bestow a power that is supposed to be a key to God himself; a power that makes its wearer God's vassal on Earth, and Satan has manipulated Zobek and the other Lords of Shadow to acquire it for his own means.

Satan has unimaginable power to wield on this Earth, and can use both Light and Shadow energy to cast destructive spells or summon demonic Reapers from other planes. However, he is not able to command his full strength while chained to the earthly plane, and thus remains weakened against Heaven's chosen.

Size

Difficulty

Items

Light Gem Medallion

Many of the Brotherhood of Light carry these magical disks. They allow the user to transform Neutral Elemental Orbs into power for Light Magic. Magical gems can be inserted into the empty slots and when all five slots are filled with blue gems, the Light Magic container's capacity is increased. Zobek gave this one to Gabriel the first time they met.

Life Gem Medallion

Warriors of the Brotherhood of Light usually wear these. Magical gems can be inserted into the empty slots and imbue the wearer with increased stamina. When all five slots are filled with green gem, the life bar's capacity is increased.

Shadow Gem Medallion

These medallions are worn only by a select few of the Brotherhood. Most fear the use of Shadow Magic and shun its application but some feel that, in order to defeat evil, one must learn both the light and dark aspects of magic. This disk allows the user to transform Neutral Elemental Orbs into shadow energy. Gems can be inserted into the empty slots and when all five recesses are filled with red shadow gems, the Shadow Magic container's capacity is increased.

Dark Gauntlet

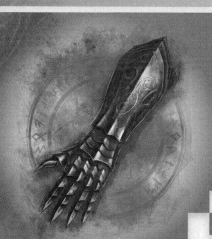

This piece of Aghartian mage-smith technology was not originally part of the design for the Black knight Golem but was somehow magically melded with the construct during the final stages of its creation. Claudia's father included it because of the sheer power and brute force that it gave the Golem and he deemed it necessary in order to protect his beloved child but, in truth, it has a much darker purpose.

Cyclone Boots

A gift to Cornell, these powerful boots were forged long ago. They allowed him to travel vast distances at a tremendous speed. However, after he became the Dark Lord of the Lycans, he improved upon their design, using Shadow Magic to turn them into a powerful weapon.

Seraph Shoulders

Carmilla, being one of the founders of the Brotherhood, received these magic shoulders as a gift from the Order for her devotion and purity of sprit. Crafted with the feather of an Archangel, originally the Seraph Shoulders allowed their wearer to fly short distances but now, after centuries of misuse by the corrupted Vampire Dark Lord, only a fraction of their true power remains.

Combat Cross Body

While most of the Brotherhood utilizes more conventional armaments, Gabriel has been gifted with the Combat Cross, a heavy iron crucifix which hides a retractable chain inside.

The cross body was one of the first relics the Brotherhood acquired centuries ago; its full origin is unclear but it is rumored to have been forged from the nails used to crucify martyrs.

Stake

The artisan who made the chain and hook tip for the Combat Cross, Rinaldo Gandolfi, wanted to give the weapon even more options for hand-to-hand combat, especially against supernatural creatures of the night. He designed the stake attachment, which eventually gave the Combat Cross the nickname "Vampire Killer."

Spiked Chain

Rinaldo Gandolfi built two different chains for the Combat Cross but one was never approved by the Brotherhood, for obvious reasons. The elders thought that the spikes were too cruel for the holy nature of the weapon. However, instead of destroying it, the artisan hid the links in one of the mausoleums of the Order, believing that one day it might be needed.

With the spiked chain, the Combat Cross can be used to saw though obstacles and to "tame" dangerous monsters by looping it around their necks.

Hook Tip

This relic was also built by the renowned artisan, Rinaldo Gandolfi. The articulated metal tip can be used to grip objects and enemies from a distance, giving the Combat Cross the properties of a grappling hook. This also allows the wielder to climb, rappel, and swing around the environments when combined with the Combat Cross.

Holy Water Flasks

At first glance, these flasks appear to be empty. However, when opened, there will always be a few drops of blessed water at the bottom. These are the endless tears of the fourteen holy helpers. They can be used to sanctify water, which, in turn, serves as an excellent weapon against creatures of the night. The bottle explodes with holy flame upon impact, which are devastating to Vampires!

Dark Crystals

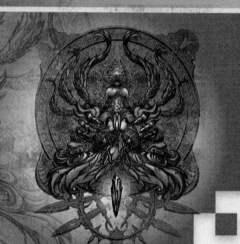

These crystalline formations are the result of a phenomenon that occurs in zones with a high concentration of Shadow energy. In these places, the land, impregnated in magic, erupts abruptly creating the characteristic geo-like patterns.

The crystals are pure Shadow Magic. They are much more volatile and dangerous than the gems from the medallions. They are so powerful that just one full crystal can be used to summon a demon from the Shadow plane.

Fairies

Fairies are a race of mystical beings that have been driven into hiding by the spread of mankind and civilization. Sometimes called the "Sidhe", they dwell in forests and meadows, hiding amongst the flowers and blossoms there. Fairies are born of the soil, and take the form of beautiful flowers before emerging as fully-grown creatures. According to legend, the Fairy Queen sometimes bestows mortals with the care and protection of the Fairy folk.

Silver Daggers

These Daggers have been balanced to be thrown with extraordinary precision. They are made of silver, and have small bones of saints hidden in their grips; both characteristics give this weapon its destructive power against supernatural beings, especially those who are descendants of the Lycanthrope Dark Lord.

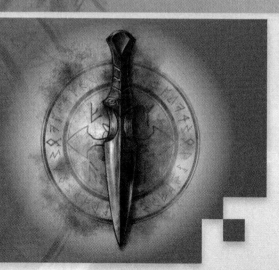

BASIC ACTIONS

Direct Attack
□ / Ⓧ

A basic direct chain attack. Will only hit enemies directly in front of you.

Area Attack
△ / Ⓨ

A basic area effect chain attack. Will hit all nearby enemies around you.

Use Secondary Weapon
◎ / Ⓑ

Use the currently selected secondary weapon by pressing the ◎/Ⓑ button. Switch between available secondary weapons with the directional buttons.

Jump
Ⓧ / Ⓐ

A basic jump. Combine this move with other attacks to perform aerial combos.

Block
Hold L2 / LB

Press and hold the L2/LB button to block enemy attacks. Unblock able attacks are indicated with a bright warming flash.

Synchronized Block
L2 / LB

Press the L2/LB button at exactly the right time to synchronize your block. When performed correctly, the enemy will be stunned for a few moments.

Dodge

L2 + L3 / LB + Left analog stick

While blocking (L2/LB) use the left stick to evade enemy attacks.

Stomp

Hold L2 + X / LB + A

Similar to dodge, but performed while airborne, this is a good defense against enemies who attack you while in the air. Landing back on the ground can also knock back smaller enemies surrounding you.

Grab & Interact

R2 / RB

Press the R2/RB button to grab enemies or interact with a glowing object. Small enemies can be thrown against other foes by moving the left stick in the desired direction while performing the grab action.

Rappel & Climbing

R2 / RB

You can navigate vertical surfaces using the Combat Cross. Press R2/RB to interact with a shining Grip Point and then use the left stick to move. Pressing ■/X or ▲/Y will kick away from the surface and pressing X/A will let go from the Grip and allow you to jump away.

Combat Focus

The combat focus is an ancient technique from the Brotherhood of Light. Once fully focused, a capable warrior can extract Neutral Elemental Orbs from his enemies after each successful hit. (Usage) The combat focus meter is filled when you fight well; use varied attacks and avoid being hit. Lack of combat will slowly decrease the meter and magic use will pause it.

Experience Points

Experience points measure the progression of you skill in the game. Points are earned by defeating enemies and solving puzzles. (Usage) The number beneath the Health Bar indicates the amount of Experience points available to spend. This will glow when you can buy a new combo from the Travel Book. You can spend Experience point in the Extras Menu to unlock bonus features.

ADVANCED MOVES

Direct Attack Combo

□/✕ x 5

A link series of direct attacks. The last hit of the sequence is a block breaker, and will expose an enemy to further attacks.

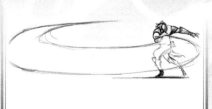

Area Attack Combo

△/Y x 8

A linked series of area attacks. Less powerful than a direct attack, but very useful for crowd control.

Rising Strike

□✕/✕ A

This direct attack will lift up smaller enemies in front of you, allowing additional attacks to be combined with it.

Rising Assault

△✕/Y A

This area attack will lift up all surrounding smaller enemies, allowing additional attacks to be combined with it.

Direct Counterstrike

□/✕ x 3

Immediately after a synchronized block, you can unleash a devastating direct counter attack.

Somersault

L2 + ✕/LB + A

While blocking L2/LB use the jump ✕/A to leap over and land behind an enemy. (Necessary relic(s): Cyclone Boots)

Guillotine Upgrade

Hold □/✕

Press and hold the □/✕ button while airborne to use this direct attack as a finisher in any aerial attack sequence. You chain will smash down on any enemies in front of you as you land. Good for dispersing ground-based enemies! Hold the □ button longer to perform an upward blow after landing the Guillotine.

Spinning Chain

Hold △/Y

Press and Hold the △/Y button while airborne to use this area attack as a finisher in any aerial attack sequence. Your chain will sweep around and hit any enemies around you as you land.

Air Grab

R2/RB

Press the R2/RB button while airborne to grab an enemy and pull them into the air. Combine this with further aerial attacks to extend the combo. This attack only works on smaller enemies.

Downward Punch

R2 / RB

If you are airborne with an enemy in the air nearby, press the R2/RB button to blast it down to the floor below you.

Flying Kick

R2 / RB

Press the R2/RB button while airborne to grab an enemy and launch into them with a downward kick. This attack only works on larger enemies.

Area Counterstrike

△ / Y x 3

Immediately after a synchronized block, you can unleashed a devastating area counter attack that affects surrounding enemies.

Direct Heavy Combo Final

Hold ▣/Ⓧ, ▣/Ⓧ x 9

Press and hold the ▣/Ⓧ button to start a sequence of heavy direct attacks. Repeated ▣/Ⓧ button presses adds further hits to the combo. This upgrade adds a final blow to the combo sequence that's also a block breaker.

Chain Barrier Upgrade

Hold △/Y, △/Y

Pressing and hold the △/Y button to start a sequence of heavy area attacks. You can control the direction of the attacks during the combo with the left stick. Enemies in front and behind can be hit with this series of chain attacks, too. With this upgrade, you can finish the combo sequence at any time with a second press of △/Y, which performs a massive final hit that's also a block breaker.

Circular Chain

▣/Ⓧ, △/Y, △/Y

A combination attack useful in many different battle situations. It begins with a direct attack, closely followed by two area attacks. Use this to attack an enemy directly while keeping others at bay.

Chain Saw

▣/Ⓧ, △/Y, Hold ▣/Ⓧ

Shred any enemy in front of you with this chain spin attack. Holding the ▣/Ⓧ button at the end of the combo extends the duration of the spin.

Ground Cutter

▣/Ⓧ, Hold ▣/Ⓧ, ▣/Ⓧ

This variation of the Chain Saw attack can be used at the end of an aerial combo sequence. Press the ▣/Ⓧ button while in the air, the press and hold the ▣/Ⓧ button a second time. Make sure you are holding the button down as you land. Finally, press the ▣/Ⓧ button one last time to launch forwards into enemies with a spinning chain attack.

Somersault Strike

▣/Ⓧ x 3

After leaping over enemies using a Somersault, immediately press ▣/Ⓧ three times to attack them from behind before they can react. (Necessary relic(s): Cyclone Boots, Dark Gauntlet)

SECONDARY WEAPONS

Throwing Daggers

◎/Ⓑ

With the Daggers selected, press the ◎/Ⓑ button to throw one towards an enemy. You can manually aim the throw by pushing the left stick in the desired direction. Daggers are particularly effective against lesser Lycanthropes, greater Lycanthropes and Wargs.

Explosive Daggers

◎/Ⓑ

With Shadow Magic active, Daggers will explode on impact. Some switches can be activated from a distance using Explosive Daggers. (Necessary relic(s): Shadow Magic)

Dagger Wave

Hold ◎/Ⓑ

Press and hold the ◎/Ⓑ button to throw multiple Daggers at one time. You can throw a maximum of 5 Daggers simultaneously.

Dark Crystal

Hold ◎/Ⓑ

With the Dark Crystal selected, press and hold the ◎/Ⓑ button to destroy it, releasing the demon contained inside. This Secondary Weapon requires four crystal shards fused together, but is powerful enough to annihilate most enemies around you, and will seriously damage even the most massive and powerful of foes. The energy within a complete Dark Crystal can be used to power certain ancient devices, too.

Fairies

◎/Ⓑ

With the fairies selected, press the ◎/Ⓑ button to release one against the nearest enemy. Additional fairies can be released by pressing ◎/Ⓑ again. Fairies will home in on their target and can distract certain enemies, allowing you time to execute a devastating attack on them. Fairies are very fragile and will die after one use. The magical forces that animate the fairies can be used to reactivate certain ancient devices.

Light Fairies

◎/Ⓑ

With Light Magic active, Fairies will explode on contact with the enemy. This explosion deals a great amount of damage and can be fatal to some enemies. However, fairies will also perish in the attack. (Necessary relic(s): Light Magic.

Holy Water Flasks

◎/Ⓑ

With the Holy Water Flask selected, press ◎/Ⓑ to throw one at the nearest enemy. Using this weapon while airborne will throw it directly downwards. Holy Water is particularly devastating against Vampires and the Undead.

Divine Shield

◎/Ⓑ

With Light Magic active, throwing a Holy Water Flask will create a magical barrier around you, which can deflect many enemy attacks, while still allowing you to move and fight normally.

MOUNTS

Ride Horse

Attacks

Press ■/Ⓧ to attack the Wargs. Press ▲/Ⓨ to attack the Lycanthrope riders. Both attacks can be aimed left or right with the left stick.

Dodge

Press and hold L2/LB button and press the left stick to either side in order to dodge incoming attacks from Lycans.

Ride Spider

Mount

Press the **R2**/**RB** button while the Spider is stunned to mount it.

Attacks

Press **□**/**X** to perform a melee attack. Press **△**/**Y** to perform a ranged attack.

Special Abilities

Spiders can use their web to interact with the world around them. Press **△**/**Y** to use the web on a glowing interactive object.

Dismount

Press and hold the **R2** and **L2**/**LB** and **RB** buttons at the same time to dismount and kill the Spider.

Ride Warg

Mount

Press the [L2]/[RB] button while the Warg is stunned to mount it.

Attacks

Press ▲/Ⓨ to slash with the claws. Press and hold ■/Ⓧ to charge a bite attack, release the button to attack.

Special Abilities

Wargs can jump further and climb better than humans. To Jump, further double-tap the left stick in the desired direction and then press Ⓧ/Ⓐ when you reach the edge. To climb, simply press Ⓧ/Ⓐ next to the glowing surfaces.

Dismount

Press and hold the [L2] and [L2]/[LB] and [RB] buttons at the same time to dismount to dismount and kill the Warg.

Ride Warthog

Mount

Press the button while the Warthog is stunned to mount it.

Attacks

Press or to perform melee attacks. Push the left stick towards enemies to charge into them

Special Abilities

Warthogs can be used as a battering ram. Press and hold the left stick in the direction of the target and charge against it.

Dismount

Press and hold the and and buttons at the same time to dismount to dismount and kill the Warthog.

Ride Troll

Mount

Press the ▣/RB button while the troll is stunned to mount it.

Attacks

Press ▣/✕ or ▲/Y to perform melee attacks.

Special Abilities

Trolls can use their mighty blows to smash heavy obstacles. Move near to the glowing obstacle and press ▣/✕ or ▲/Y to attack it.

Dismount

Press and hold the ▣ and ▣/LB and RB buttons at the same time to dismount to dismount and kill the Troll.

RELIC POWERS

Light Magic

Attacks made while Light Magic is active will replenish your health, at the cost of Light Magic energy.

Usage: L1/LT

Press the L1/LT to activate or deactivate your Light Magic powers.

Magic energy absorption: L3/R

Press and hold the L3/R button to gather surrounding Neutral Elemental Orbs into your Light Magic Container.

Shadow Magic

Attacks made while Shadow Magic is active will inflict more damage, at the cost of Shadow Magic energy.

Usage: R1/RT

Press the R1/RT to activate or deactivate your Shadow Magic powers.

Magic energy absorption: L3/R

Press and hold the L3/R button to gather surrounding Neutral Elemental Orbs into your Light Magic Container. You can collect both types of magic types of magic at the same time, pressing both sticks together.

Relic Moves List

Tremor Punch

L2/LB + Hold ▢/X

A powerful forward punch. Charge up by holding the L2 and ▢/LB and X buttons until your Dark Gauntlet glows red, then release for extra devastation. This attack can knock back enemies in front of you, or even kill them in one shot. The Tremor Punch can also activate certain mechanical switches. (Necessary Relic(s): Dark Gauntlet)

Earthquake Punch

L2/LB + Hold △/Y

Powerful downwards punch. Charge it up by holding the L2 and △/LB and Y buttons until your Dark Gauntlet glows red, then release for extra range and power. This attack can knock back enemies surrounding you, or even kill them in one shot. The Earthquake Punch can also activate certain mechanical switches. (Necessary Relic(s): Dark Gauntlet)

Sprint

L3 x 2

Double-tap the left stick to perform a sprint. While you are sprinting, you can jump longer distances. (Necessary Relic(s): Cyclone Boots)

Shoulder Charge

Hold L2/LB + Left Stick

With Shadow Magic active, you can power up your charge into an attacking move. The shoulder charge can also be used to smash through weakened doors and walls. Check for the telltale sign of falling dust and debris. (Necessary Relic(s): Cyclone Boots + Shadow Magic)

Flame Dragontail

L2/LB + X/A

Dark Gauntlet assisted uppercut. This attack will lift up many nearby enemies, allowing you to continuing the combo with additional aerial moves. (Necessary Relic(s): Cyclone Boots + Dark Gauntlet)

Double Jump

X/A x 2

Tapping the jump button twice in quick succession will allow you to jump again in mid-air. Use it to reach new heights or change the trajectory of your jump. (Necessary Relic(s): Seraph Shoulders)

Holy Jump

Ⓧ/Ⓐ x 2

With Light Magic active, a double jump will unleash beams of Light energy around you. The first attack made against a blinded enemy inflicts bonus damage, but removes the effect. (Necessary Relic(s): Seraph Shoulders + Light Magic)

Sprint Thrust

L3 x2 ▲/Ⓨ, ■/Ⓧ

Finish off your sprint with a blast attack. Double-tap the left stick and then press ▲/Ⓨ followed by ■/Ⓧ when you are close to your enemy. The closer you get to your target the more effective this attack will be, often knocking even the mightiest foe to the ground. (Necessary Relic(s): Cyclone Boots)

Light Flash

L2 / LB

A synchronized block while Light Magic is active will detonate a flash of magical light that will blind nearby enemies. The first attack made against a blinded enemy inflicts bonus damage, but removes the effect. (Necessary Relic(s): Light Magic)

Landslide Punch

L2 / LB + Hold ■/Ⓧ

While you are airborne, use this attack to swoop back down to the ground with a huge Dark Gauntlet punch. Press and hold the L2/LB and the ■/Ⓧ buttons, charge the Gauntlet for as long as you can, and the release to set off the attack. (Necessary Relic(s): Dark Gauntlet)

Avalanche Punch

L2 / LB + Hold ▲/Ⓨ

While you are airborne, use this attack to throw a wave of Dark Gauntlet power downwards. Nearby smaller enemies will be lifted into the air, allowing you to continue the combo with further attacks. Press and hold the L2/LB and the ▲/Ⓨ buttons, charge the Gauntlet for as long as you can, and then release to set off the attack. (Necessary Relic(s): Dark Gauntlet)

Erosive Chains

■/Ⓧ, Hold ▲/Ⓨ

With Light Magic active, this combo extends a cage of whirling chains around you. The cage draws surrounding enemies into it, while also damaging them and replenishing you health. (Necessary Relic(s): Light Magic)

Shadow Flames

▲/Ⓨ, Hold ■/Ⓧ

With Shadow Magic active this combo creates a flaming vortex of Shadow energy from you Combat Cross. This fire is extremely deadly, but you will be rooted to the spot while you use it and it cannot be adjusted mid-stream, so line up your enemy carefully. (Necessary Relic(s): Shadow Magic)

Flame Claws

L3 x 2 ■/Ⓧ

Use the Dark Gauntlet while sprinting to throw several claws of damaging Shadow Magic energy towards your enemy. With your Shadow Magic active, Double tap the left stick to begin the sprint, then press the ■/Ⓧ button at any time to use the Flame Claws. (Necessary Relic(s): Shadow Magic, Dark Gauntlet, Cyclone Boots)

Upward Guillotine

■/Ⓧ, Ⓧ/Ⓐ x 2

Using the Seraph Shoulders to double jump this attack can lift enemies in front of you much higher into the air than the Rising strike combo, creating more time to perform additional attacks on them. (Necessary Relic(s): Seraph Shoulders)

Whirlwind Flap

△/Ⓨ, Ⓧ/Ⓐ x 2

Using the Seraph Shoulders to double jump this attack can lift enemies all around you much higher into the air than the Rising Assault combo, creating more time to perform additional attacks on them. (Necessary Relic(s): Seraph Shoulders)

Air Wave Flap

L2/LB, Hold △/Ⓨ, △/Ⓨ

After lifting enemies into the air with a Dark Gauntlet uppercut, you can flap the Seraph Shoulders to repel them away from you with this combo. Good when surrounded or in a tight spot to buy time! (Necessary Relic(s): Seraph Shoulders, Dark Gauntlet)

Holy Cross

△/Ⓨ, Hold ☐/Ⓧ

With Light Magic active, this combo creates a dazzling blaze of light energy from your Combat Cross. This glare can blind and damage any enemy caught in its beams, but you will be rooted to the spot while you use it, so select you target carefully. (Necessary Relic(s): Light Magic)

Exploding Quake

☐/Ⓧ, Hold △/Ⓨ x 2, Hold △/Ⓨ

With Shadow Magic active you can call forth a series of fiery explosions from the earth beneath you enemy's feet. The final eruption will release a larger shockwave against all nearby enemies. Tap the ☐/Ⓧ button, then press and hold the △/Ⓨ button until you smash the Combat Cross against the floor to start the combo. Each subsequent △/Ⓨ press will create and additional explosion, climaxing with a final press and hold of the △/Ⓨ button the last devastating attack. (Necessary Relic(s): Shadow Magic)

Ultimate Light

Hold L2/LB, Ⓛ

Press and hold the L2/LB button to activate the Ultimate Light Mode. While you are in this state you will spin constantly, attacking any surrounding enemies. You can use the left stick to aim the spin in order to deal the maximum amount of damage. However, be aware of your Light Magic supplies! (Necessary Relic(s): Light Magic)

Ultimate Shadow

R1/RB, Ⓛ

Press and hold the R1/RB button to activate the Ultimate Shadow mode. While in this state, the left stick will make the character perform powerful charge movements in the desired direction. (Necessary Relic(s): Shadow Magic)

Walkthrough

CHAPTER I

LEVEL ONE: BESIEGED VILLAGE

A storm is coming. Mankind faces ruin and despair. The world is changing, yet hope remains in the hearts of the people. We go about our daily lives never knowing the forces that can change our destinies forever; we are oblivious, ignorant like sheep to the slaughter. This night in the year of our Lord 1047, marks the beginning of our journey together; a journey into darkness, into madness. I watch him from the shadows. Is he the one? He has come far already but he will be tested; tested to the very limits of human endurance…and beyond. This night he rides looking for the old gods, armed with an amulet that has led him here; tonight he will begin his journey into oblivion.

Monsters

‡ Lesser Lycanthrope   ‡ Great Warg

Relics

‡ Silver Daggers

Unlockable Trial

‡ Finish the level, defeating the Great Warg with at least one surviving villager.

Walkthrough

Battle the Lesser Lycanthropes

To conquer the Lycanthropes in the sodden village, read the many introductory tips carefully and put them into action. Practice your Direct and Area Attacks as well as combinations of these two while also throwing jumps into the mix for a plethora of attack combinations.

HEALTH FONT

Look for and use the Health Font with its glowing green energy vapors found to the left of the gate. Walk up to the healing statue and press the Grip/Use button to accept its gift of life.

SILVER DAGGERS

Continue the battle with the pack of Lycanthropes while experimenting with various attack combinations. Notice that the Lycanthropes begin dropping **Silver Daggers**. Daggers can also be found by breaking various objects. Currently you can only hold five Daggers at a time, which is the amount of one dagger pickup. Grab them before they disappear. A successfully thrown dagger can completely eliminate one Lycanthrope.

GRAB ATTACKS

Two targeting halos appear around your enemies when you Grab them. Hold them until the outer ring enters the center ring. Once the outer ring is enclosed inside the center ring you can press any button to unleash a Grab attack on your enemy. Once you have them, you can use the left stick to throw them in any direction inflicting major damage.

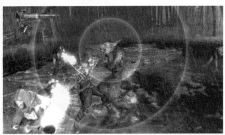

TRAVEL BOOK

Soon you are prompted to check out your Travel Book. You use this book (accessed by pressing the SELECT or BACK) to buy new combat moves and abilities. It also holds information about Castlevania and its inhabitants. You can spend some hard-earned Experience points on a new move now.

After defeating all the Lycanthropes in the village a Great Warg smashes through the gate and attacks. The battle begins with its mighty jaws bearing down on you as it has you pinned down to the ground. Quickly and repeatedly press the attack button indicated on screen to escape its hold. The button for this type of mini-game changes each time.

As soon as you break free from the Warg's maw, come up swinging to issue some damage before the enemy is ready to attack again. Block when the Great Warg swings its mighty claws. Block and Dodge when the beast glows with a bright light. The very moment after a dodge is the best time to attack; you will be beside or behind the enemy.

Continue to dodge every attack the beast throws at you, then attack with various combos. Wear the beast down until its health is emptied (the boss's health appears in a bar in the top right corner). The Great Warg retreats for a short time, taking a position on a nearby boulder. He is preparing to pounce again for another round.

A large post lying in the mud at Gabriel's feet glows with attention-getting effervescence. As soon as control returns to you, Grab the post at your feet and position it towards the leaping Great Warg so that the beast impales itself upon it. This quickly ends the battle and the Great Warg's life.

QUEST REVEALED

After the battle is won, Gabriel speaks with a rattled villager. You explain that you are seeking the Guardian of the Lake and reveal a glowing amulet. The villager tells you *he* will find *you* in the forest.

 **Level Completion**

At the end of each level you receive stats from the Travel Book. Here you can review what difficulty mode the level was completed in, what type of monsters were defeated, what kind of relics were found, and how many Experience points you currently have.

Newly unlocked Artwork is also noted. It can be viewed in the Extras section of the Main Menu. You now have another opportunity to purchase new skills through the Travel Book. If you continue your quest, the World Map is revealed. By reselecting the previous level completed you can discover new Trial Unlocks. By returning to previously visited levels you can try to beat new challenges to reach 100% completion.

LEVEL TWO: HUNTING PATH

I follow him into the old forest watching him from afar, he is strong indeed. The one God comes to drive out the many but here, in this place, God's influence is thin and threadbare. The old gods still hold sway here. Few venture this far into the wood. He is disturbed by dreams, dreams that gnaw at his very soul. He will rest for the night, but rest will not come easy. The battle has left him weakened. He knows the dream will return, and though he fears nothing on this Earth, his nightmares sap the strength within him and leave a cold grip on his heart. Tomorrow he will use the old hunting path, long has it been in disuse, but for now…he dreams.

Monsters

‡ Lesser Lycanthrope ‡ Warg

Hidden Items

‡ 1 Life Magic Gem

Unlockable Trial

‡ Finish the level after killing at least 50 Goblins.

Walkthrough

First Horseback Forest Battle

Waking from a dream concerning his departed wife Marie, Gabriel is approached by a magical talking horse. Soon they are racing through the forest together being closely pursued by Wargs and Lycanthrope riders.

Use normal attack and dodge maneuvers to battle the enemies as they approach you on either side. Direct Attacks damage Wargs while Area Attacks damage the Lycanthrope riders. Inevitably, you'll be knocked to the ground. No matter how long you stay mounted, you always end up in the same section of forest.

WOUNDED LYCANTHROPE

During the chase sequence, you can jump mounts. Once a Lycanthrope is wounded, press the Grab button while the Lycanthrope is glowing to climb on the Warg and finish its rider.

Forest Path Lyncanthrope Battle

Battle the Lycanthropes while walking back (towards the camera). Inspect the left side of the pathway to find a defeated knight lying on the ground. Grab the **Life Magic Gem** from his body. This is sadly the only Magic Gem in this level. You need five of these to fill a Life Gem Medallion, which increases the capacity of your life bar. You can find four more in the next level.

DIRECT COUNTERSTRIKE

While battling the pack of Lycanthropes practice your newly discovered skill: Direct Counterstrikes. The first step is to block just as the enemy is striking you. After performing a synchronized block press the Direct Attack button three times quickly to unleash a devastating counterattack.

Second Horseback Forest Battle

During the second horseback challenge you are again confronted with Lycanthrope riders on galloping Wargs. You can continue this challenge segment as long as you wish. You'll have opportunities to execute kills with the focus ring feature, but, eventually you fall from your horse into the second forest clearing.

Second Forest Clearing

As soon as you begin the battle with the Great Warg and Lycanthropes in the second forest clearing, rush over to the Health Font on the right side of the path. Fully recover your health, then start taking out the enemies. The cursed beasts don't mess with you while you replenish health from a Health Font. Make full use of your new Direct Counterstrike ability while laying waste to Lycanthropes using daggers.

After defeating the pack of enemies in the second clearing, your horse once again rides out of the forest thickness to rescue you at a moment of despair. With Great Wargs nipping at your heels, you quickly close in on two Great Wargs blocking a broken earthen bridge ahead. Your magic horse makes the death defying leap over the gorge, disappears midflight leaving just enough velocity for you to land on your feet on the other side.

EXPERIENCE POINTS

At this point you should have accumulated a decent amount of EXP. Be sure to check the Travel Book every once in a while for new combos and movements to spend these points on.

LEVEL THREE:
THE DEAD BOG

Alone again with only his thoughts as company, he continues on his journey to find the one he seeks. Who or what was the strange creature? There is a power here that few know, a power that could have some influence on events. Perhaps the guardian of the lake is aware of him now and offers aid in his quest? There is just the small matter of the Dead Bog to overcome, a place that has claimed the lives of many of the Brotherhood. The smell of death is strong here and danger lies around every corner, but nothing will stop him...nothing will stand in his way.

Monsters

‡ Goblins   ‡ Swamp Troll

Relics

‡ Hook Tip

Hidden Items

‡ 4 Life Magic Gems

Weapon Upgrade

‡ Dagger Upgrade + 5

Unlockable Trial

‡ Finish the level without recovering health by any means.

Walkthrough

Through the Thickets

Push through the narrow, thicket-laden canyon, to find a fallen knight's corpse on the left as you reach the first clearing. Grab the **Life Magic Gem** from the knight. Just yards away is another knight lying flat on the ground. Grab the Brotherhood Knight **Scroll** from his corpse. You can read this scroll in the Travel Book. The knight warns of the beasts in the bog water, and grants you his knowledge to avoid them.

Use the ledges near the second dead knight to navigate around the obstruction. Push around the corner and leap to the final piece of ledge. Drop down into the next clearing.

Goblin Bombs

You are instructed on how to pick up and throw back Goblin bombs when you reach the second clearing. Basically, you stand over a thrown bomb and grab it. The throw is automatic. The *small* Goblin bestiary is unlocked after slaying your first small Goblin. Goblins are just about as tough as Lycanthropes and they can throw bombs. You can make a Goblin drop a bomb by grabbing them and pressing any button when the white targeting rings glow in the center ring. This causes the Goblin to drop a bomb, so make sure to pick it up quickly and toss it back...or if you aren't going to use it, make sure to clear away to avoid the explosion.

The last Goblin appears in a cinematic. You hit him with a knife throw, which pushes him into the bog water. A small Naiad bubbles beneath the surface and reaches up and grabs the unsuspecting Goblin. The Naiad bestiary now appears in your Travel Book.

Crossing Bog Water: Noxious Poison & the Naiad

The next task that lies before you is crossing the Naiad infested bog water. Before you just jump in headfirst, look closely at the bog water. Notice the dark areas of the green bog water. The darker, fog-free area of the water is your target pathway. You can walk through this area to your target platform without taking poison damage. However, this area is usually home to a few Naiads. The foggy areas of the water are poison clouds. You can only survive for a short time walking through these toxic areas. Your life bar shakes, then begins to drain if you remain in the noxious areas of the water.

Pay close attention to the water effects in the bog: you usually have time to escape a Naiad if you walk through disturbed, wavy ripples; however, if you walk through bubbly water you can pretty much count on a nasty encounter with the Naiads. It's not over if grabbed by a Naiad; if you can hit the beast when the center target ring glows white, then you can kill the Naiad and safely move on.

First Bog Fork

The first clear path through the bog water leads you to a small island in the middle of the poisonous lake. From here you can cross a shallow area on the right and follow the stone stairs off down the right fork, or pass through the dark green bog water path on the left to reach a Health Font and a left fork path. These paths eventually meet and **Life Magic Gems** can be found down each path, so doubling back before you reach a point of no return is required to get all the Magic Gems. A **Life Magic Gem** can be found on a small rock platform in the bog water down the left path.

If you take a right at the fork mentioned above, after dropping off the second pathway drop ledge, double back along the right side and you can find a cave. Inside the cave is a dead knight with a **Life Magic Gem**. Prepare to fight Goblins; they follow you into the cave.

Tree Bridge

When you reach the Goblin camp with the large dead tree, use or bounce two Goblin bombs at the rotted tree. With two successful bomb attacks, the tree falls over and creates a bridge to the next area.

Find the **Scroll** on the dead knight on the first small island in the bog water beyond the tree bridge. This describes the mausoleum with a secret relic inside.

BOMB BLOCK BREAKERS

Gob grenades are normally obstruction breakers. If you perform a synchronized block on a thrown grenade, the grenade is deflected to the highest valued target in the nearby environment.

The Last Fork before Mausoleum

Continue to follow the bog and you'll reach one last fork before a set of stairs that lead upward to a hill on the left. You'll encounter more Goblins at the foot of these stairs. Lead the Goblins down the right fork and battle the Goblins near the Health Font. When all is clear, return to climb the stairs to the mausoleum on the hill.

Mausoleum

Circle around to the left side of the mausoleum at the end of the bog. Here you'll find ledges to climb to reach the broken rooftop. In a cinematic, you jump into the mausoleum through the hole in the roof. Approach the altar inside to claim the Hook Tip enhancement for your Combat Cross.

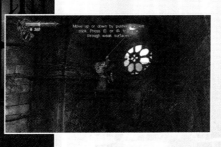

The articulated metal tip can be used to grip objects and enemies from a distance, giving the Combat Cross the properties of a grappling hook. This also allows the wielder to climb, rappel and swing around the environments when combined with the Combat Cross.

Use the Combat Cross to grapple onto the shiny Grip Point above the round window in the back of the mausoleum. Climb up the rope until you are at equal height as the window, then use either attack button to bust through the window. This begins a boss battle out in the connecting graveyard.

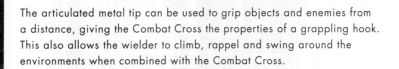

Boss Battle:
Swamp Troll

The creature that's been following you through the bog has now caught up to you in the graveyard behind the mausoleum. The Swamp Troll is an enormous creature and a rare subspecies of the larger Cave Troll. Although similar in appearance to their dry land cousins, the thick fur has been replaced with a slimy coating. Swamp Trolls are ferocious in battle and display a cunning that belies their outward appearance.

FLYING KICK

Purchasing Flying Kick before starting this battle. Press the Grab button while airborne to grab an

enemy and launch into them with a downward kick. This attack only works on larger enemies.

The Swamp Troll uses the many statues around the graveyard as weapons. It can also create a ground shockwave that can damage you at long distances if you are on the ground at the time of the attack. Jump into the air to avoid this attacks.

Use Flying Kick attacks with any combination of attacks you are comfortable with. Be sure to Dodge to weaken the Swamp Troll. When its health is almost depleted, it becomes stunned for a short time. When this happens it glows a bright white. This is your cue to approach it and use a grab move. Successfully hit the creature three times in a row as the targeting rings appear in three consecutive mini-game sequences. Each successful hit results in a bone-crunching knee kick to the beast's head.

SMASHING HEADSTONES

Smash headstones and statues to uncover hidden Silver Daggers.

The fourth successful mini-game attack has you leaping on top of the monster's head and prying the beast's mouth with your Combat Cross.

With the monster defeated you earn 250 EXP! Before you leave the area, open the Brotherhood Ark to find a secondary weapon upgrade. This upgrade increases your Silver Dagger capacity from 5 to 10. Now use the Hook Tip to grapple onto the Grip Point in the tree and swing out of the graveyard.

Exiting the Dead Bog

Follow the pathway out of the graveyard to a set of large stone steps. If you continue around to the back of the graveyard you can find a Health Font. Replenish your health, then climb to the end of the broken stairs.

From here to the exit on the distant mountainside are a series of ledge grabs and ledge shimmies mixed with an equal amount of Grip Points to use your new Hook Tip for rappelling and climbing. The challenge starts with a leap across the first gap to reach the first ravine spire.

FIRST ROCK SPIRE

The next challenge is to drop and grab onto the edge of the first spire. Drop down a few ledges and work your way around the corner before the ledges crumble at your fingertips. Once on the other side of the spire, notice the glowing Grip Point, but don't use it yet. Instead, continue further toward the protruding ledge beside you by jumping to the next grip ledge. Drop down to the ledge with the dead knight and take the last **Life Magic Gem**. Now return to the Grip Point. Use the Grip Point to drop to the lower ledge (still on the first spire).

SECOND ROCK SPIRE

Jump from the lowest ledge on the first spire to the second spire. Climb the series of rock ledges until you can use a high Grip Point to climb to the top ledge on the second spire. Latch onto the side of a ledge on the spire and move around the corner, drop on the highest ledge and find yet another Grip Point up higher on the spire. This grapple allows you to swing and jump to the top of the third spire.

THIRD AND FOURTH ROCK SPIRE

Jump from the top of the third spire to the fourth (the one with the broken arch). Jump from the end of the fourth spire to the lower fifth spire with the dead tree growing out of it.

FINAL LEDGE: OPPOSITE MOUNTAINSIDE GOAL

From the fifth spire (with the dead tree growing out of it) you can find a Grip Point on the final ledge. Swing and climb up using this Grip Point. Get to the top of the ledge and follow the stairs into the mouth of the cave to complete the level.

LEVEL FOUR:
PAN'S TEMPLE

The search of the bog fades into memory and a land of great beauty lies before him, a paradise where nature lives in harmony with all living creatures, indeed a refuge for those who wish it. He is close now, close to the old gods and the old ways. Long forgotten by men, this kingdom was once revered by all, yet now only a small part remains. Soon even this will disappear. The amulet senses its master; its journey is almost over. He will need all his strength now, all his wits if he is to succeed here, if he is to convince the old god to help him.

Hidden Items

‡ 1 Life Magic Gem   ‡ 5 Magical Runes

Weapon Upgrade

‡ Holy Water Upgrade + 2

Unlockable Trial

‡ Finish the level after beating Pan's trial in 5 movements

Walkthrough

Lush Forest

You have entered the heart of the forest where Pan, the faun who protects it calls his home. There's no combat in this level, just a couple secret areas to find. Begin the adventure by grabbing the **Magical Rune** on the left side of the forest pathway near the beginning. Once taken, the rune fills the first slot in the magical rune amulet displayed on the right side of the screen.

At the point where the camera spins around and you end up running toward the camera, you'll find another **Magical Rune** on the right side of the pathway (Gabriel's left).

Just yards away from the second Magical Rune you can cross over to the right side of the pathway by traversing over a large tree root. Here you'll find a dead knight propped up against the same root. Take the **Scroll** from the body. The scroll is a reminder to continue to search dead knights for the possibility of more Magic Gems.

At the U-turn in the path, just beyond the knight you can find some birds perched on a large rock in the lower right corner of the screen. Look for the very bright, yellowish green vegetation that's bathed in light. Push into that area until the camera swings around. You'll find the third **Magical Rune** there.

Continue through the narrow pathway beyond this rune location and you'll quickly come to a corpse face down in a shallow pool of water. Take the **Life Magic Gem**. Return to the previous pathway.

Continue around the large U-turn in the pathway and find the fourth **Magical Rune** where the pathway darkens and narrows to its most restricted point. Find a **Scroll** on the corpse at the end of shallow pond just before the tree tunnel. This is a letter from the dead knight Victor to his wife. Continue through the tree tunnel to reach another clearing.

In the clearing, you'll find an unreachable Brotherhood Ark. Just ahead of the Ark and on the right you can find the fifth and final **Magical Rune** to complete the collection.

HOLY WATER UPGRADE + 2

When you earn the Seraph Shoulders, return to this level and perform a double jump here to reach the high ledge with the Brotherhood Ark to obtain the Holy Water Upgrade + 2.

Pan's Trial

A fairy appears and hovers in the oval green light at the end of the forest trail. This happens once you find all five of the Magical Runes and activate Pan's Amulet in the same location. To proceed, you must match the order of the rune symbols above the fairy's head to the Magical Rune symbols in your display on the right side of the screen. Select a Rune Slot with the left stick and change it using the Direct Attack button. When successful, the fairy breaks the green barrier allowing you to continue.

Through Magical Rune Protected Tunnel

Once through the tunnel beyond the Magical Rune puzzle, take the narrow pathway leading up on the left side of the forest wall. Follow this winding pathway until you reach Pan's Temple.

Pan's Temple

In a cinematic, Gabriel calls for Pan to show himself. Gabriel pleads that the Brotherhood needs his help. Pan materializes and claims to be the guardian of the Lake of Oblivion, where the living can communicate with the dead. Gabriel informs Pan that they have been deserted by God. Creatures from the void come to claim the souls of men, to wipe mankind from the face of the Earth. The elders believe that God has abandoned them and that a powerful spell has been unleashed by someone or something. They also dreamed that a message waits for Gabriel here at the Lake of Oblivion. Gabriel was instructed to seek Pan out in hopes that he could show Gabriel the path. He believes that his wife that was murdered two days ago is waiting here to deliver a message to Gabriel. Pan helps if you first pass his test.

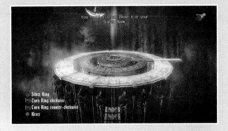

Pan's Trial

You enter a large chasm with a large machine made up of three large rings. Your wife Marie lies in the middle of the puzzle with a large swinging blade above her. Since she's already dead, this shouldn't bother you. As control returns to you a **Scroll** enters your inventory. It's a hint Scroll. The Scroll informs you that you earn 200 EXP upon completion of the puzzle and illustrates the rules of the challenge.

To reach Marie before she dies you must find a path to follow. Try to overcome your sorrow and you may avoid her demise. Choose only one direction. You can also cheat and use an unlock solution accessed in the hint scroll, but by doing this you lose the puzzle's award. It says "choose only one direction in which to turn the three wheels and their shine will reveal the hidden path of self redemption."

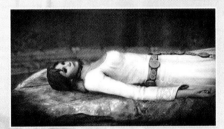

To work the puzzle you select a ring with the left stick, turn a ring clockwise with the Grab / Use button and turn counterclockwise with the Block / Dodge button. Reset the puzzle using the Area attack button.

Just know that the paths (or bridges) need to connect to one another to allow you cross the gaps between each ring to get to your wife. Here is the five-move solution:

‡ Turn the center ring clockwise	‡ Turn the outer ring counterclockwise
‡ Turn the center ring clockwise	‡ Turn the outer ring counterclockwise
‡ Turn the middle ring clockwise	

After completing the challenge and saving your wife, you suddenly stab her in the gut during a cinematic and turn to face the camera. Your face is covered with a fragmented metal mask. You awake from the scene while standing beside Pan once again. You ask what the vision means and he replies only that you are worthy of entering the Lake of Oblivion. Pan allows you to pass through his temple and reminds you to pack daggers; you'll need them.

LEVEL FIVE: OBLIVION LAKE

The test has shaken him. I see the doubt in his eyes as he heads towards the lake. So Pan is helping him now? That's good. Perhaps it bodes well. I wonder if he knows what awaits him here, in this place where the dead can contact the living. It is cold now. A chill wind blows through his heart; I can see it. Feel it! He will need help if he is to succeed. He must not fail. He will not fail, not now...not yet, not if I have anything to do with it.

Hidden Items

‡ 1 Life Magic Gem

Relic

‡ Light Gem Medallion

Monsters

‡ Ice Titan

Unlockable Trial

‡ Finish the level and defeat the Ice Titan in less than 1:30 minutes

Walkthrough

Frozen Lake

Walk out to the broken angel statue standing before the frozen lake. Find a **Life Magic Gem** on the corpse near the statue. Walking out onto the frozen lake triggers a boss battle.

Boss Battle: Ice Titan

Buried deep below the surface of an ancient lake, waiting to be found, are the remnants of a once great European civilization, among them, a Titan of War! Before Rome, before ancient Greece, this great empire possessed technology that surpassed all others, and this Titan marks the pinnacle of their achievements. A great conflict known as "The Necromantic Wars" obliterated this once thriving civilization and this great feat of engineering was lost. When the dark spell that isolated the heavens from our earthly plane was cast, the souls of the dead were drawn to this place and somehow gave new energy to the magic runes, reanimating the Titan one final time...

Boss Attacks

The Ice Titan has two ranged attacks that you should avoid at all costs: one sends a shockwave through the ice that cannot be blocked, and must be dodged laterally. The other creates a magic symbol in the ground around which many ice stakes emerge, trapping you inside an ice shard prison. Only the Titan can destroy this ice prison with a punch.

Battle Strategy

To defeat the Titan you must climb onto it, destroying the runes that empower the statue. There are a total of four runes, distributed across the colossus body.

First Rune

The first rune is on its left arm. To climb onto it, you must get it stuck in the ice. Get close to the colossus; it will try to hit you by punching down. If the Titan hits twice in the same spot in the ice, it will break beneath it, trapping the arm for a few seconds. You must take advantage of this time to use the Hook Tip on the trapped arm and start your ascension (look for the highlighted emblem to grapple to).

Once you start to climb, the Titan tries to rid you by shaking its arm. You must press and hold the Grab button to cling onto the colossus surface, or you fall down. Find the clearings in each ring of its arm to continue further up the arm by leaping and latching onto the crevices between the stone sections of the arm. The first rune is high on the back of its arm. Once you reach the first rune, press the Direct Attack button to destroy it. Hit it repeatedly until it shatters.

10 HITS!

Each Rune takes 10 Direct Attack hits before it is destroyed.

Second Rune

Angered, the Titan then raises his arm and tries to swat you with its other hand. Dodge this by jumping just before the impact, and use the Hook Tip on the right hand (you'll see a large section of its right hand glow). Quickly, grapple to the chest plate (this too will glow brightly) where the second rune is located.

While destroying the second rune, the colossus again tries to hit you, this time using his left hand. You must dodge these attacks by side jumping when you see the gigantic hand coming.

Third Rune

After shattering the second rune, another Grip jump takes you to the monster's back. This Grip Point is located on the end of the Titan's pointy chin. You swing from the chin to the back of the head. Climb over and smash the rune in the middle of his upper back while dodging overhead hand grab attempts.

Fourth Rune

Grapple from the back up to the glowing area of the Titan's head. Move your way around the head to the right ear area. The Ice Titan scratches the zone where you are while also trying to shake you off. Smash the final rune ten times to complete the challenge.

The colossus finally hits you, throwing you onto the ice. Fortunately, you are saved just in the nick of time by another Brotherhood Knight, Zobek.

Gabriel's wife appears to give him a message from the Order that founded the Brotherhood, but the message is still yet unclear to her. Zobek shares a prophecy with Gabriel. It is written that a pure-hearted warrior will claim the power of the Lord of Shadow as his own and use it in order to overcome all evil. Zobek convinces Gabriel that they could actually bring Marie back from the realm of the dead. They decide to split up as to not draw attention to themselves. Gabriel will head through the land of the Lycans while Zobek will leave for the territory of the Vampires.

Zobek hands you a gift to help you on your travels. The **Light Gem Medallion** allows you to absorb spiritual energy and will help cure your wounds.

CHAPTER II

LEVEL ONE: ENCHANTED FOREST

We part ways, he and I. My instincts tell me he is filled with hope, a hope that will drive him ever onwards. Good. Perhaps he is the one, a warrior of pure heart who can deliver us from all evil…perhaps. I wonder what went through his mind when he saw her there, his beloved. Did he see his dreams, or did he see his future blown away like leaves on the wind? I spy him as he heads out toward the reaches of Pan's influence. A forest that leads to the land of the Lycans lies to the east. The ruin of an ancient civilization is there, forgotten and decaying. Once a proud testament to man's ingenuity and vision, it has now been conquered by Nature, as she claims all things for her own.

You have unlocked a main character entry.

Hidden Items

‡ 1 Life Magic Gem

Weapon Upgrade

‡ Dagger Capacity Increase

Monsters

‡ Goblin	‡ Warg
‡ Lesser Lycanthrope	

Unlockable Trial

‡ Finish the level after killing 30 Goblins with their own grenades

Walkthrough

Leap of Faith

Zobek's character entry is added to your Travel Book once you begin this level. To continue ahead into the Enchanted Forest, you must make a leap of faith by dropping over the edge of the cliff below the crooked tree. The camera angle then changes, and you'll find yourself on a short ledge above a waterfall.

Work your way down the waterfall cliff by dropping down to a lower ledge and then using the two Grip Points to swing down to a lower walkway-type ledge. Find a **Scroll** on a dead knight on this walkway. In the scroll, the knight says he gave his Life Gem to his comrade, so be on the lookout for this.

Continue down the ledges, hop across the river near the leaning tree, and continue down the ledges on the opposite side of the cliff until you reach a save point at the bottom at the stream level.

Waterfall Tunnel

If you enter the stream and follow it to the cave behind the waterfall, you find a device in the back of the cave that can only be triggered using Shadow Magic. You must return here when you have that skill. Once you return, the Brotherhood Ark contains a dagger upgrade.

Neutral Elemental Orbs

Follow the path around and over a dead tree trunk. Destroy the single Lycan that rushes out of the forest. This creature leaves behind Neutral Elemental Orbs. Thanks to the Light Magic Medallion that Zobek gave you, you are able to absorb these orbs.

Press and hold the Absorb Light Magic button to absorb the orbs before they disappear. The energy fills a new gauge that appears at the bottom left corner of the screen. This is your Light Magic Container. Press the Light Magic Enable / Disable button to switch on your Light Magic power. This causes you and the container to glow dark blue.

Attacking enemies with Light Magic switched on replenishes your health. However, your Light Magic Container depletes. Furthermore, enemies do not drop Neutral Elemental Orbs while you have magic on. You can only get the orbs by killing enemies with your magic off.

Drop off the side of the pathway to a lower path where you soon find a Neutral Elemental Energy Statue. You can use this to restore your magic levels.

Use your newfound magic while taking out the Lycanthropes that cross the stair-like rock pathway. This attack is triggered when you move beyond the large tree root in the path just beyond the energy statue. Notice your health rising as you defeat the enemies while Light Magic is turned on. After this battle, refill your magic using the statue, and then continue on down the path.

Ancient Ruins

When you reach the city ruins, the path splits two ways. Find the stairs on either side of the rear fountain. Use either one, as both ways lead to the next zone.

RIGHT PATH FROM ANCIENT RUINS

The right path is the easier of the two. It begins with a gap that you must jump across. After crossing to the other side, you reach a dead end. The only way to continue is to solve a simple minigame in which you pull from the tree until it bends, allowing you to use one of its branches to grapple across a crag using a higher ledge Grip Point. This is where the two paths cross.

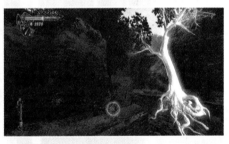

LEFT PATH FROM ANCIENT RUINS

The left path from the ruins goes through an exhausted water channel. Some Goblins assault you along the way, but the attacks cease after one or two waves. After defeating them, you reach a save point. You can also find a bag of 10 daggers in this area.

The channel ends in a vertical wall that you must climb. Use the Grip Point on the right wall to reach a series of ledges to move along while hanging by your arms. At the top of the waterfalls, you'll find a dead knight with a **Scroll**. The Scroll is an account of the end of his journey.

Cross the small arched bridge to the area to the right. In this area, head toward the camera and drop down to a lower ledge near a statue. Continue toward the camera to find another ledge with a Grip Point. This is where the left and right paths cross.

Joined Paths

Look for a dead tree located down below the ledge below the Grip Point (the puzzle reached at the end of the right path). A dead knight with a **Life Magic Gem** lies below the tree in a shallow stream. Defeat the nearby Goblins and follow the shallow stream to a nook where you can climb rubble to a pathway where the dead tree puzzle is located.

Grapple to the tree branch and press the indicated button quickly to break the branch off. This reveals a couple Grip Points: one on the dead tree and another on a nearby ledge beyond the tree. Use these to reach the other side of the crag.

Both paths end on this upper plateau at a solid rock wall beyond the arched little bridge. To pass through, you must use the Grip Point on the top of the wall. While in the grapple stance, kick the wall to propel against it and break the crumbled area near the top on impact.

Focus Scroll

Through the high, breakable window, you'll land in a courtyard where a dead knight lies holding the Focus Scroll. Take the Scroll. The combat focus is an ancient technique from the Brotherhood of Light. Once fully focused, a capable warrior can extract Neutral Elemental Orbs from his enemies after each successful hit. The combat focus meter is filled when you fight well: use varied attacks and avoid being hit. Lack of combat slowly decreases the meter, and magic use pauses it. The Focus Bar is shown at the bottom of the screen during combat. Light all of the runes by fighting well.

Warg Focus Tutorial

Battle the Warg that appears in this courtyard. Use varied attacks and try not to get hit to quickly fill up the Focus Meter. Once the meter is full, maintain your focus, and the enemies will drop Neutral Elemental Orbs after each successful hit, allowing you to maintain your magic supplies during combat or until you lose focus. Switching your magic and getting hit interrupts focus. When you defeat the Warg, a Goblin ambush occurs.

Goblin Ambush

Battle the Goblins and throw any dropped grenades at the large, glowing exit doors. Use grab attacks to make the Goblins drop grenades. Try to perform synchronized blocks on thrown grenades to deflect them into the target door. Continue slaughtering the beasts and throwing grenades at the door until it is blown open, which only takes two successful hits.

The Great Dekuh

Look for a giant tree stump in the center of the next area. This is the entrance to the spider dwelling underground. The dead stump is so big that it can only be reached from the ledge on the left side of the area behind the Great Dekuh tree stump.

You can find a dead Knight with a Scroll on the right side of the stump. This **Scroll** tells of the Great Dekuh tree.

Jump and climb the wall on the tower behind the tree stump, and the camera soon shows a Grip Point at the top of the tower. Grapple up and clamber along the top ledge with your hands to reach the opposite side of the tower. The camera moves to reveal a Grip Point on the end of a protruding beam. Use the Hook Tip on it and then release to land on a high ledge near a tree. Find the Grip Point on a tree branch and use it to swing into the top of the large tree stump to end the level.

LEVEL TWO:
UNDERGROUND CAVES

He is becoming stronger with every step he takes; his prowess in battle is undeniable, he will need it now. Goblins are one thing, but there are other creatures in the dark places of the world, creatures who know nothing of his plight but fight for their very survival. Many fallen brothers are testament to this; indeed, their bleached bones adorn the tortuous tunnels in this godforsaken place. He runs ever onward into peril. I wonder who their prey is and who is the hunted; perhaps when the time comes these creatures will know fear as they look into the eye of their quarry. Go my friend, save your love!

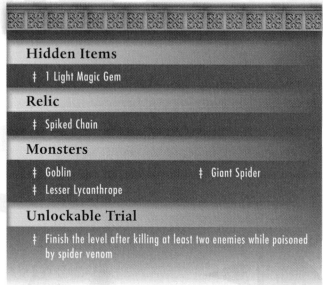

Hidden Items
‡ 1 Light Magic Gem

Relic
‡ Spiked Chain

Monsters
‡ Goblin   ‡ Giant Spider
‡ Lesser Lycanthrope

Unlockable Trial
‡ Finish the level after killing at least two enemies while poisoned by spider venom

Walkthrough

Inside the Great Dekuh

Enter the small cave at the bottom of the tree stump landing area. Follow the cave to a small waterfall. Drop down to latch onto the edge of the ledge. Using your hands, crawl left along the thin ledges until you receive a message instructing how to jump backward while hanging. This places you in the spider's den. In a creepy cinematic, the Giant Spider creeps up behind you and attacks just as you turn around to face it.

Great Spider

You begin this battle with the Great Spider trying to chew your head off. As soon as you recover character control, repeatedly press the displayed button to avoid the poisonous bite.

Move as much as possible to avoid the webs from the spider, or you will be entangled in them. If you are entangled in a web attack, quickly and repeatedly press the indicated button to break free.

Furthermore, if the spider poisons you, quickly use the Light Magic Power to stop losing health.

Attack the spider with varied attacks to raise your focus meter and eventually make it produce orbs. Hit it with everything you got to take it out as quickly as you can. These monsters are the largest type of known arachnids, and they are much more aggressive than any of the normal-sized varieties of spider. Once defeated, the Giant Spider is added to your Travel Book's bestiary.

Use the Grip Point at the upper end of the connecting tunnel to escape the spider's den. Do not drop down once you reach the next cave wall; instead, climb up to the Grip Point. You can pull up onto a ledge and enter a new tunnel above.

Lesser Lycans and Spider

At the end of the cave, grapple down to a large cave below with scattered ruins and skeletons. As soon as you touch down, Lesser Lycanthropes attack. Take out a few Lycans, and soon a Giant Spider joins the battle. Keep moving and take out the Lycans as quickly as you can so you don't have to battle them along with the spider. Learn the spider's attack pattern, learn to dodge when necessary, and be patient as you battle.

Cave Exploring

After defeating the spider and the Lycans, jump up on the ledges in the back right side of the cave and enter the next. On the entry ledge, you'll spot a Grip Point on a ledge near your feet. Drop down over the edge of this ledge so you can catch the groove. Release and then quickly use the Hook Tip to latch onto the Grip Point. This must be done quickly, or you'll drop to your death.

Grapple down to a lower ledge that you can shimmy across to the right. At the end of this ledge, jump to the right to reach the next ledge. Climb up onto the top of the ledge and run along the narrow path heading to the right.

Jump the gap at the end of the narrow ledge and then cross the thin, yet strong, spiderweb bridge. If you begin to lose your balance on the web, you can use the Grab button to regain balance and then continue crossing to the next tunnel. A dead knight with a **Scroll** is located at the end of the web bridge, at the mouth of the tunnel. This Scroll hints that you can actually ride spiders like you would a Warthog and that the webs are strong enough to bear the weight of a grown man.

Continue through this cave, then drop down to the open area outside. This area forks off into two directions starting with web bridges. For now, it is advised to cross the leftmost web bridge and enter the tunnel entrance on the following ledge. Through the next cave, you'll continue into another open area. Continue following the ledge through another short tunnel, toward the camera. Once you reach the next sun-bathed rock ledge, you'll find a save point.

Tough Totem

In a gap in the pathway, you discover a totem that you cannot break until you upgrade your Combat Cross. This occurs shortly, and then you can return and uncover the totem's secrets. Leap up to the top of the continuing path and enter the next tunnel.

First Mausoleum Key: Grenade Door

Another locked door similar to the one you found at the end of the last level is at the end of the pathway. Seems you'll need grenades or something strong to break these doors. If the Goblins in this area do not appear on your first time through, travel down the left path as far as possible, receiving the next **Scroll** from the knight on the ledge and then returning to trigger the Goblin battle.

Defeat the attacking Goblins and use their grenades to destroy the nearby sealed door. Use grab moves and attack the foes to make them drop grenades. A few direct hits with grenades, and the door will be destroyed. Beyond the destroyed door, find the first **Rune Stone Key** on the knight on the edge of the ledge through the short tunnel.

Second Mausoleum Key

Return the way you came, past the unbreakable totem, and enter the large cave where the first web path fork is located. Now, take the right path by crossing the web bridge to the rightmost ledge.

Defeat the Giant Spider on this ledge. Climb the series of ledges starting on the right side of this ledge. Shimmy over to a wider ledge, jump up on it, and walk across. Jump over the gap to reach a ledge at a tunnel entrance. Head through the tunnel.

Use your Hook Tip on the Grip Point on the tunnel ceiling to overcome the waterfall gap in the tunnel. Swing across the gap and find a dead knight at the mouth of the tunnel. This ledge overlooks the locked mausoleums where you soon use these two rune keys. Take the **Rune Stone Key** from the knight and drop off the ledge and head to the locks flanking the locked entrance of the mausoleum.

Mausoleum

Activate the Use button while standing near the two shields on either side of the mausoleum's locked entrance. The Rune Stone Keys are sucked into the lock mechanism, which then unlocks the front door. Enter the mausoleum.

Second Holy Relic: Spiked Chain

Inside the mausoleum, you'll find another altar. Just as you did in the first chapter when you acquired the Hook Tip, insert your Combat Cross. This time, you imbue the cross with a **Spiked Chain** enhancement. Rinaldo Gandolfi built two different chains for the Combat Cross, but this one was never approved by the Brotherhood, for obvious reasons. The elders thought that the spikes were too cruel for the holy nature of the weapon. However, instead of destroying it, the artisan hid the links in one of the mausoleums of the Order, believing that one day it might be needed.

Destroying the Totem with the Spiked Chain

With the Spiked Chain, you can use the Combat Cross to saw through obstacles and to "tame" dangerous monsters by looping it around their necks. This upgrade is necessary to open the path to the end of the level: a glowing totem blocks the web-filled cave beyond the Spiked Chain altar. Walk up to the totem and press the Use button. Gabriel automatically wraps the chain around the totem, and then you must follow the left stick's back and forward motion prompts to destroy the totem. The level exit is through the tunnel. Before you leave via one last Grip Point jump, read the tip below.

TOTEM PULL

Before you exit the level through the tunnel you unblocked in the mausoleum, head back to the previous totem to use the Spiked Chain on it. This reveals a tunnel that leads to a dead knight on a ledge. This knight holds a **Light Magic Gem**.

LEVEL THREE:
LABYRINTH ENTRANCE

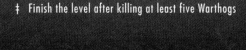

Hidden Items
‡ 1 Light Magic Gem

Weapon Upgrade
‡ Fairy Upgrade + 2

Monsters
‡ Goblin   ‡ Lesser Lycanthrope
‡ Greater Lycanthrope   ‡ Warthog

Unlockable Trial
‡ Finish the level after killing at least five Warthogs

So, he has found another of Gandolfi's upgrades? This was unforeseen, though it should prove useful in the challenges to come. The lost city of Agharta looms before him. I wonder if you know what truly lies ahead for you, Gabriel...what God has in store for you? The land of the Lycans! This ruined city now belongs to their Lord, and you can be sure he will not allow you to pass without forfeiture of your life. But in order to bring her back, you need to defeat him, my friend. You need to crush him into the dust...like the worm that he is.

Walkthrough
Riding the Warthog

You begin this mission standing in the cave exit, overlooking the Lycanthrope labyrinth's entrance. Drop down into the area below and approach the locked gate. A screen prompt hints that Goblin grenades cannot destroy this gate.

After you inspect the door, some Goblins and a Goblin riding a Warthog attack. Instead of trying to take out all the Goblins and the Warthog, try just damaging the Warthog until it becomes stunned. The Goblin rider on the Warthog must be destroyed. Once enough damage is done to the Warthog, the monster starts glowing to indicate a possible interaction with it. Press the Grab button from a short distance to mount the beast.

While on the Warthog, press the Direct or Area attack buttons to perform melee attacks. Push the left stick toward enemies to charge into them. Now, take out all the Goblins in the area. Remain on the Warthog until you've defeated all waves of Goblins. If they take out your mount, another Warthog appears (which you must stun and mount to progress).

CHARGE ATTACK

When mounted on a Warthog, it is usually safer to attack enemies with the Warthog's charge attack than it is to battle with its melee attacks.

With the Goblins gone, move toward the camera and get a running start at the locked gate. A good fast collision with the Warthog's head into the gate can take the gate down. Now you can choke your mount by pressing the Grab and the Block buttons at the same time.

The Labyrinth Walls

Just through the destroyed gate and to the right lies a dead knight holding onto a **Scroll**. The Scroll simply describes the dead knight's turmoil in this area.

Travel left down the pathway until you reach the back left corner, where a pile of rubble in the pathway meets the old, castle-like walls of the labyrinth. You can find a ledge to jump up to in this nook. Shimmy around the left inside corner, and then jump to the top of the ledge. Here, you'll find a Grip Point near the top of the wall. Grapple to the top of the wall and hop over to the inside of the decrepit labyrinth.

Inside the Lycanthrope Labyrinth

Carefully walk across the scaffold along the right wall of the Labyrinth to reach a dead knight holding a **Scroll**. He leaves a good tip behind: if you block often, you can increase your focus. This allows you to focus much quicker, which enables you to keep magic on all the time during combat.

LIGHT MAGIC GEM

Before you get to the dead knight mentioned above, look for steps that lead down, which are to the right of the cross planks. They are hard to spot from above. Continue down the stairs to find a hidden Brotherhood knight lying in a small room. He holds a **Light Magic Gem**.

From the dead knight with the Scroll at the end of the scaffold, turn back and take the left path toward the central column. Jump up onto the glowing ledge and shimmy around the corners to the opposite side of the column.

Continue to shimmy around the corner where the large outstretching beam connects to the column. Drop down onto the lower ledge over the gap. Drop off the left end of this platform to latch onto the glowing edge. While hanging there, you'll spot a Grip Point on a high broken beam above your head. Grapple to this point.

While swinging high on the rope, press the Attack buttons to push away from the wall and then press the Jump button to let go at the correct time to land on the next ledge to the left. Follow the stairs down into a lower pit, where a Lesser Lycanthropes battle occurs.

Lesser Lycanthrope Battle Arena

The Lesser Lycanthropes should not pose a serious threat. However, to exit the area, you must use the mechanism present there, a fact that complicates combat against the enemies. To use this door crank device, just get close to it and press the Use button. When you grab the handle, use the left stick to rotate the mechanism and open the door slowly from bottom up. You must use the time between Lycanthrope waves to open the door, or they interrupt the process.

Once the door is completely opened, it remains raised, and you can pass into the next area. As you do, a quick cinematic shows a Lycan being grabbed by the throat by something much bigger and then being pulled off screen. When control returns to you, you find yourself facing a long, wide exterior passage with many statues near multiple waterfall fountains.

Find a **Scroll** on a dead knight on the right side. It mentions that each species is weak against a particular weapon. Follow the path to the hallway entrance. If you walk toward the camera, you can find a bag of daggers.

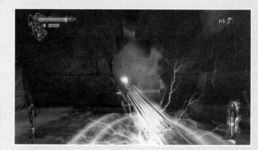

Waterfall Tunnel

If you enter the stream and follow it to the cave behind the waterfall, you find a device in the back of the cave that can only be triggered using Shadow Magic. You must return here when you have that skill. Once you return, the Brotherhood Ark contains a dagger upgrade.

Exit the hallway and drop into the arena. Once you arrive, a wave of Goblins attacks. Notice that one picks up and holds on dearly to a strange looking horn. This is the instrument you need to work the door mechanism. Your task is to recover this bull's horn from the Goblin and use it on the device. You cannot attack while holding the horn, so it's a good idea to defeat all the Goblins before trying to open the door. In addition, any hit received makes the character drop it, allowing another to pick it up.

Once all the Goblins are destroyed, a Great Lycanthrope enters the arena. Use many dodge maneuvers and keep moving as you hit this beast with your most powerful attacks. Once you defeat this large Lycan, you can freely open the door. Pick up and place the bull horn in the bull head device by walking up to it with the horn in hands. Press the Use button again to place the horn in its correct position. Turn the device clockwise to open the door. While you are opening the door, one of the ropes supporting the stone wall fails, letting the door crash against the floor and breaking it. You fall through the hole created in the arena floor.

LEVEL FOUR: WATERFALLS OF AGHARTA

This ancient city occupies many layers, each one being the foundation for the next. It is a labyrinthine maze of dead ends and forgotten walkways. Danger lurks around every corner. He has shown great resilience, but this journey will take him longer than anticipated and deeper than any man has ever ventured in centuries. He will need all his wits to find an alternative route into the heart of the city...where his destiny awaits him!

Hidden Items
‡ 2 Light Magic Gems

Relic
‡ Shadow Gem Medallion

Monsters
‡ Giant Spider
‡ Greater Lycanthrope
‡ Lesser Lycanthrope
‡ Cave Troll
‡ Small Troll

Unlockable Trial
‡ Finish the level after killing at least 20 Small Trolls while you are mounted on a big one

Walkthrough

Entry Point

Gabriel has fallen through the floor of the upper labyrinth; he now stands in a subterranean passageway, which continues underneath the labyrinth ruins. Begin this level by picking up the **Scroll** from the dead knight beside you. You learn that this knight was on a quest to become invincible by collecting enough Magic Gems. The Scroll mentions a nearby Light Gem. Follow the pathway through a short tunnel on your right. When you reach the next cavern, jump across the large gap to reach the next large plateau. Here, you will battle a Giant Spider.

Giant Spider Battle

As you explore the new plateau, a large, crooked tree across the ravine begins to glows. When control returns to you, a single Giant Spider attacks. Use dodge maneuvers and your favorite spider-tactics to wear the beast down. Again, if you are poisoned, switch to Light Magic to stop the loss of health.

Beat the Giant Spider down until you stun it. Mount the Spider as you would a Warthog; press the Grab button when close to the beast. Once aboard, you can press the Direct attack button for melee attacks and the Area attack button for ranged attacks. Spiders can use their webs to interact with the world around them. Press the Area attack button to use the web on a glowing interactive object. To dismount and strangle the spider, press and hold the Block and Use buttons at the same time.

Turn the spider and face the crooked, glowing tree. Shoot a spiderweb at the tree using the Area attack button, and then repeatedly press the button indicated on the screen to pull the tree toward you. The tree cracks and leans into a position a little closer to your ledge. Dismount and kill the spider. The Giant Spider drops a **Light Magic Gem**. Pick it up. Then, use your Hook Tip on the Grip Point on the tree branch to reach the distant ledge.

Leap across a gap and then drop down off the left end of the ledge at the first rock wall dead end. Shimmy around to the inside of the nook on the other side of the obstruction. Leap across the gap and pull yourself up to the next pathway.

Greater Lycanthrope Battle

Climb up to the upper pathway and follow this to a broken rock bridge. Use the Grip Point on the high tree branch to swing to a large ledge, where you must battle a Greater Lycanthrope. Break the large pottery to find daggers on this ledge. Use a grab attack to stab the Lycan multiple times with the sharp end of your Combat Cross. Follow this with repeatedly pressing the indicated button to pop his neck with your foot.

Jump up and latch onto the grooves on the canyon wall in the corner of the ledge where you battled the Greater Lycan. Jump up to one more groove above, and a Grip Point high on the canyon wall appears. Use the Hook Tip to latch onto it. Move the left stick sideways to gain momentum, and when you are on the leftmost pinnacle of your trajectory, jump. If done correctly, you'll safely land on the next platform.

Leap across the gap at the waterfall and enter the following tunnel. A short cinematic shows the scope of the next large cavern. Pass through the tunnel and do battle with the Greater and Lesser Lycanthropes in the next clearing.

Concentrate on avoiding the Greater Lycan while eliminating the Lesser Lycanthropes. With that done, you can concentrate on the one-on-one battle with the big Lycan. Do everything you can to whittle its health down so you can stun it, and then perform a grab attack on it like you did on the previous Greater Lycan. After the battle is won, you can freely explore the battle platform. Find the **Scroll** on the dead knight lying against the left end of the ledge. The Scroll is a reminder to revisit levels after acquiring new skills and weapons to find more hidden goodies.

Cliff Face

Use the Spiked Chain on the large face statue found on the side of the cliff, which is over the next gap at the end of your current platform. Repeatedly press the indicated button to pull the weak statue from the side of the cliff. The debris forms a makeshift bridge.

As you walk across the newly formed rock bridge, a Grip Point appears on the canyon wall. Grapple from the Grip Point and then scale downward to the area below the Grip Point. You'll reach a new level of the environment where many more ledges and waterfalls can be seen.

Head to the right along the new pathway. When you leap up to the first ledge, you reach a save point. Walk to the outer right edge of this ledge and seek out another Grip Point in the distance to the right. Latch onto this distant post and swing to the new platform where a Troll battle is initiated after a cute little cinematic ends.

Troll Battle

The cutscene ends with you being ambushed and grasped by a large Cave Troll; this initiates a quick minigame. Press the displayed buttons repeatedly to get free from the Cave Troll's grip. The Cave Troll tries to grab you again if you fight too close to him. The Cave Troll has a ground pound attack similar to the Swamp Troll you fought so long ago. Jump to avoid the shockwave.

To continue, you must ride on the Cave Troll and use its strength to destroy the remaining small Trolls and then the large boulder that blocks the way off of this platform; stun the Troll (beat it down to an inch of its life), press the Grab button to mount on it, and then use any of its attacks against the small Trolls.

The Direct and Area Attack buttons perform melee attacks. To smash large glowing objects, you just need to approach them and press the Attack buttons. The strangling dismount is performed in the same manner as with other mountable beasts. After defeating all the Trolls and breaking boulder, kill the Troll and use the Combat Cross on the newly discovered Grip Point.

Two-Tunnel Fork

You reach a large ledge with a Health Font and two tunnels. The tunnel on the right is not a continual path, but it leads to a nice item waiting for you. It's best to travel through the right tunnel first and then return to the fork to continue through the left tunnel.

Right Tunnel: Light Magic Gem

The tunnel on the right seems to lead nowhere, but if you look behind the waterfall in the path, you can find another Brotherhood knight with a **Light Magic Gem**. Return to the Health Font and head down the left tunnel to continue the quest.

Left Tunnel

A totem blocks the tunnel on the left. Use the Spiked Chain on it to advance towards the next area. Head through the tunnel and jump the gap to the next large battle ledge. Here, you'll battle Lesser Lycanthropes with one large Greater Lycan. Take out the small Lycans first and then beat the larger one down until you can perform the grab finishing move attack on it.

After you've destroyed all of the Lycans, continue toward the left side of this platform, where you can use some ledges in the middle of the waterfall to hop to the opposite side. The climbing zone ends shortly after, with a grapple climb that leads into a new arena. This new arena is where you battle a Giant Spider.

Giant Spider Battle

A cutscene plays in which you see a spider crawling over a wooden bridge, which falls under its weight. With the bridge gone, the only possibility is to build a new one, using spiderweb.

A single Giant Spider appears, which must be used to build a web bridge (if you kill this enemy, a new one spawns). You must beat the spider's health down to pretty much nothing before it is stunned. Once the spider is glowing and stunned, approach it, mount it, and press any button when the ring crosses the center targeting ring to successfully tame the beast. Once you're mounted on it, the directional attack makes it launch some web goo forward; aiming towards the opposite side of the bridge triggers a cutscene in which the web bridge is created.

SPIDER WEB ATTACK

This attack can stun other enemies if it hits them, although it won't cause much damage.

The new web bridge cannot sustain the spider with Gabriel mounted on it, so you must kill the monster and dismount before continuing across the bridge.

The Mausoleum

The path on the other side of the bridge leads to an old mausoleum. Inside the mausoleum, you find a wooden totem that you can saw down using the Spiked Chain. Behind it, lying in the center of the small room, there is a dead Brotherhood knight; if you get close to him and press the Use button, Gabriel takes the **Shadow Magic Medallion** from his chest, enabling the use of Dark Magic.

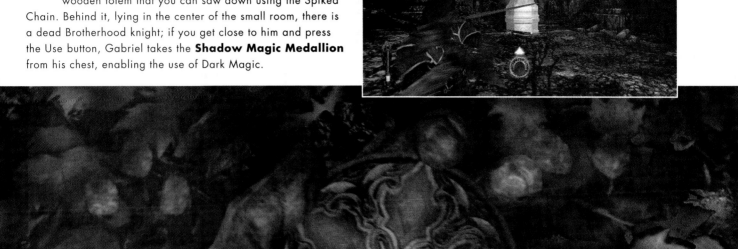

You must use Dark Magic to continue advancing, so head outside again to refill both magic meters in the nearby Neutral Elemental Orb fountain. To gather Shadow energy, press and hold the right stick button. You can recharge both magic types at the same time by pressing both sticks at once.

You might have noticed before a head shaped wall ornament, next to the exit door in the mausoleum. These magic locks must be opened with a combination of Light and Shadow magic energy. In this case, you must charge it with Shadow magic and then interact with the lock by pressing the Grab button.

Lycanthrope Battle

After leaving the mausoleum, you have the opportunity to use your new powers on some enemies, the Lycanthropes in the next chasm. Remember to switch between Shadow and Light magic to inflict more damage and recover health, respectively.

When all enemies are dead, only a climbing area separates you from reaching the end of the level—some simple jumps and a pair of Grip Point jumps that takes Gabriel back to the upper level of the Labyrinth. The last Grip Point may be hard to find, as the brightly shining sun makes the Grip Point's glow less vibrant. It's on the beam jutting out of the top of the last canyon wall on the right. You'll spot it when you reach the highest point on the climbing wall.

LEVEL FIVE: AGHARTA

Agharta was once one of the greatest cities of the ancient world, but it didn't take long to fall under the onslaught of the Dark Lord. The Lycans were innumerable and the city was razed to the ground. The Necromantic Wars, as they were known, destroyed the advanced technologies that the Aghartians had closely guarded. Eventually, the Titans fell, and then the people were massacred one by one or were turned into beasts subservient to their new conqueror. None now remain to tell the tale…

Hidden Items

‡ 1 Life Magic Gem   ‡ 2 Shadow Magic Gems

Weapon Upgrade

‡ Dagger Upgrade + 5

Monsters

‡ Lesser Lycanthrope   ‡ Small Troll
‡ Cave Troll   ‡ Warg

Unlockable Trial

‡ Finish the level without using Shadow Magic energy

Walkthrough

Claudia

Gabriel starts the level continuing the last grip jump he performed in the previous level. In a cutscene, he barely reaches the other side when a Troll surprises him. A mysterious girl saves him. Her name is Claudia, and she appears more times in the next few levels.

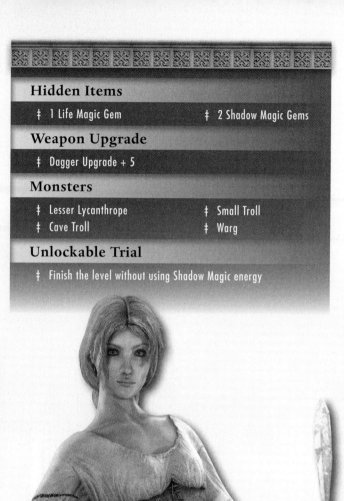

Mysterious Crystal Weapon

Did you see the crystal Claudia used to destroy the Troll? Take note of it; is a powerful weapon, which Gabriel receives later on.

After a cutscene depicts Claudia climbing the gigantic well, control returns to you; you cannot follow her right now, so you have to find another route, which in this case is the path on the right side—the broken bridge can be jumped over using a grip jump, and after that, the path splits.

EASY ROUTE

Like in the case of the spider cave, the route described here is the shortest way to get through the level, but not the only one. Explore the rest of the map to access secret areas.

Across the bridge, you discover a dead knight on the left side of the path. Take his **Scroll**. The Scroll is the knight's prayer to discover the secret to riding beasts. Defeat the attacking Lesser Lycans.

Head up the set of stairs to the left and follow the path toward the camera. Here, you'll find another downed knight with a **Scroll**. This one urges the reader to search for all the secrets in the city and reminds you that silver daggers work wonders on the Lycan.

Warg Riding

To continue, head to the rightmost zone and jump over the gap using the Grip Point found above the gap. This takes you to a new closed zone, with a ruined wooden bridge.

First of all, get close to the wooden bridge and interact with it. This attracts the attention of a Warg, which enters the arena. Now attack it until stunned, and then mount it (pressing the Grab button).

JUMPING WARG

To jump with the Warg, double tap the left stick to sprint and then press the Jump button when near the edge of a platform. If your timing is correct, the Warg jumps forward, crossing any distance to the other side.

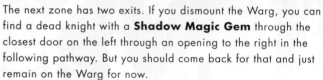

The next zone has two exits. If you dismount the Warg, you can find a dead knight with a **Shadow Magic Gem** through the closest door on the left through an opening to the right in the following pathway. But you should come back for that and just remain on the Warg for now.

Without dismounting the Warg, defeat the Lycans in this area. Notice the heavy glowing statue in this area where you battle the Lycans. Use the Troll to knock down the statue, or return here when you can Gauntlet Punch or Shoulder Dash to break the statue. Snag the **Dagger Upgrade** inside the small room behind the statue.

Enter the second passage on the left under a stone arch, where you find another Warg jump. After jumping a second time, you need to get rid of the mount to climb the wall through the open nook in the back right corner of the dead end.

Mounting a Troll

This wall jump puts you in a small arena where you are attacked by small Trolls and one large Cave Troll. You can ignore the smaller ones and focus on the Cave Troll, as you need its strength to break your way through the ruins and to quickly and effortlessly destroy the small Trolls.

Once you get the big Troll stunned, ride on it and jump down to the zone below. You next enter an arena with more Lesser Lycanthropes. Get rid of them and guide the Troll to the large, glowing metal gate blocking the exit.

After destroying the gate, dismount and move forward. You can keep the Troll but it cannot jump while under your control, so the stairs prevent you from continuing.

SERAPH SHOULDERS: MAGIC GEM

Exploring this area while not on the Warg lets you find a small yard behind a building with stair access. If you use Seraph Shoulders in the backyard, you can double jump over a broken wall and find a dead knight holding a Life Magic Gem. There's also a Health Font beside him.

Another Warg Ride

TThrough the new area, there are a set of steps that lead up and a set that leads down. The down steps lead to a belt of daggers. Head right to ascend the stairs to the new battle arena. You must find the groove in the nook to hang and jump up to the arena plateau. Just as in the previous arena, the path is obstructed. Large chasms open that seem to be the only exit, and with no Grip Points, another solution must be devised.

As soon as you enter the arena, approach the broken bridge on the left. A Warg appears and attacks; its jumping skills will be more than enough to cross the abyss, so attack it until is stunned, then mount on it like you did with the Cave Troll. Defeat the attacking Lycan and then jump the broken bridge.

If you return here when not on the Warg, you can find a dead knight in a nook behind the crooked trees near the second bridge (to the right of the second bridge jump). This knight holds a **Shadow Magic Gem**.

This path takes you back over a few more broken bridges and toward the start of the level. Gabriel's acrobatic skills were no match for Claudia's before, but now, mounted on a Warg, things are different. The monster can easily climb some surfaces that Gabriel cannot. Just press the Jump button when near a glowing wall of thick vines. After climbing to the top of the well, dismount and clamber down using the ledge and the Grip Point. As you descend, the level ends.

LEVEL SIX: DARK DUNGEON

Who is this strange girl? Surely she could not have survived alone in this hellhole? Gabriel follows her deep into the depths of the city. I wonder where she is leading him. It is strange. I hear no words, and yet it seems Gabriel is communicating with her in some way…Something tells me she has a part to play in all of this…

Hidden Items

‡ 1 Light Magic Gem ‡ 2 Shadow Magic Gems

Monsters

‡ Gremlin ‡ Giant Spider

Unlockable Trial

‡ Finish the level without using a Grip Attack against a single Gremlin

Walkthrough

Down the Well

Gabriel starts the level near the top of the well hanging by the Hook Tip on the Grip Point latched onto in the previous level. Drop down a bit, below the glowing ledge on the left. Use momentum and jump left, toward the glowing fracture in the wall. Latch on and shimmy left, jumping backwards in the waterfall gap, and then use the two consecutive Grip Points above to get across the well.

Hanging from the ledge on the other side of the well, continue moving right, jump the gap, and then use the Grip Point above to enter grapple stance again.

The next jump can be tricky: without descending more than one or two steps, propel against the wall, pressing any one of the Attack buttons, and jump toward the narrow platform in the middle of the well.

Run left and jump the gap to grip onto a glowing ledge. Shimmy left and jump the waterfall gap. Continue shimmying left until you reach a corner with another Grip Point. Grapple down and drop onto the platform below...

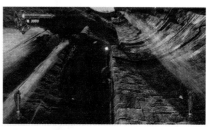

WALL JUMP FOR A MAGIC GEM

If you want to get a secret gem, do not drop down to the platform below while hanging on the last Grip Point by your chain. Slide all the way down on your chain and then wall jump backwards to grip onto a ledge behind a waterfall. Two more Grip Points swing you through an arch and leave you hanging on the side of a cracked wall. Run on the wall heading to the left and jump off the chain to a ledge where a dead knight holds a **Light Magic Gem**. Use the next Grip Point to the left to continue the quest on course.

GABRIEL WILL HELP

While moving through climbing areas, remember that Gabriel seeks out potential jumps, looking backwards or sideways when an available jump is nearby.

The Dungeon Bridge: Part 1

To the left of the stairs, you can find a dead knight with a **Scroll** inside. The Scroll speaks of a Shadow Gem a comrade possesses. As you climb the stairs, a blue light flickers on from the side of the stairs. Continue up into the next cave. Soon after venturing into the cave, Claudia appears again in a cutscene; she smiles at Gabriel and jumps across the gap—like before, Claudia's agile movements cannot be mimicked, so you must find a way to follow her.

The two large monoliths in front of you have a mechanism similar to the ones seen in the spider cave. These can be used to create a passageway that allows passage, but first, you must find the two keys that activate them.

KEYS

Every time that you are asked to find "keys" like these, slots for the needed items are shown in the interface in the top right corner of the screen. This lets you know how many items you need to solve the associated puzzle.

To get the first key, take the path on the left side of the cave. Another dead knight lies just beyond another blue light and on the left side of the pathway. Retrieve his **Scroll**, which gives tips about flammable Gremlin guano.

Gremlins!

The cavernous zone ends with a small platform where a new enemy is introduced: the Gremlins. These small and mischievous flying demons can use their slings to throw you flaming stones, but they are pretty weak and fragile overall.

FLYING CREATURES HATE DAGGERS

Against flying creatures like the Gremlins, the daggers are formidable weapons. Don't forget to use them in occasions like this.

The gremlins protect the first **Stone Rune** Key, so pick it up from the dead Brotherhood knight and go back toward the cave entrance to place it on either one of the monoliths.

SHADOW MAGIC GEM

Find the small pathway in the rocks just beyond and to the right of the dead knight holding the first Stone Rune Key. In a little cavern, locate a dead knight holding a Shadow Magic Gem.

The Dungeon Bridge: Part 2

After you use the first Stone Rune Key, half of a bridge hidden beneath the stone reveals itself, allowing you to cross half of the gap. If you move toward it, the camera focuses on a ledge on a lower level of the dungeon. A blue torch lights up near the cave entrance. Jump off the end of the bridge and enter this cave.

The second key is harder to get; Gremlins try to stop you again, but this time, they are accompanied by Giant Spiders. The new cavern is smaller, with a locked door at one side. To open it, you need the strength of a spider. First, you have to tame it (after you stun the spider, press the Grab button to start the minigame sequence).

Once you have the monster under your control, aim at the metal door and use the ranged attack button to entangle it with web, and start the resistance minigame. After you break open the door, go to the other side to pick up the second bridge key. Run back to the remaining Stone Rune keyhole while staying ahead of the flock of Gremlins hot on your tail.

Gremlin Battle

Insert the Rune Key to complete the bridge. Battle the many flying Gremlins. Cross the bridge and follow it to the dead end cavern, where you'll find a Health Font. Climb the vines and find the Grip Points and shimmy ledges to reach the top of the cave.

WALL JUMP FOR A MAGIC GEM

If you want to get a secret gem, do not drop down to the platform below while hanging on the last Grip Point by your chain. Slide all the way down on your chain and then wall jump backwards to grip onto a ledge behind a waterfall. Two more Grip Points swing you through an arch and leave you hanging on the side of a cracked wall. Run on the wall heading to the left and jump off the chain to a ledge where a dead knight holds a **Light Magic Gem**. Use the next Grip Point to the left to continue the quest on course.

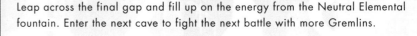

Leap across the final gap and fill up on the energy from the Neutral Elemental fountain. Enter the next cave to fight the next battle with more Gremlins.

This time, the Gremlins are fiercer and attack in even greater numbers. After some fighting, Claudia appears again with a powerful new companion; he is the Black Knight, her protector. After the introductory cutscene, the level ends successfully.

LEVEL SEVEN: SANCTUARY ENTRANCE

Fate has played its hand, and now the die is set. I knew this child would play her part somehow and it seems Gabriel has real help at last. It bodes well for our quest. The Golem that protects the girl has something that could prove very useful in the end…something unforeseen. My dear friend, I see your destiny before me, and it is terrible indeed, and yet I have trust that all will be as I have hoped.

Hidden Items	
‡ 1 Light Magic Gem	‡ 1 Shadow Magic Gem

Weapon Upgrade

‡ Dagger Upgrade + 5

Relic

‡ Dark Crystal

Monsters	
‡ Greater Lycanthrope	‡ Cave Troll
‡ Lesser Lycanthrope	

Unlockable Trial

‡ Finish the level after absorbing 20 Neutral Elemental Orbs simultaneously

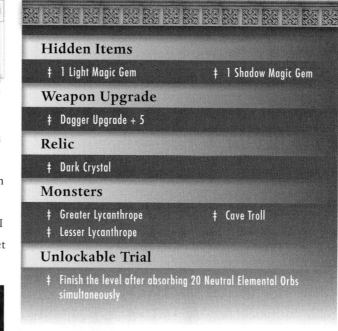

Walkthrough

Introduction

The level starts with a cutscene in which Claudia tells Gabriel her story and the tale of the Black Knight. She also describes the history of the city and how the monster's attack turned it to ruins.

You recover the control in a large area; as Claudia has said, you need a complete power crystal to activate the statue that opens the door. You need four Crystal Shards to complete one power crystal.

Forging a Crystal

To create a complete power crystal from scratch, you need to merge four single pieces into one. These pieces are scattered around the map, hidden amongst the ruins.

First Crystal Shard

Start by walking toward the camera in the first area, and you'll find some stairs to the left as the camera swings around. Exit the initial area; you need to use a Grip Jump to hop over some debris on the ground. With this action, Gabriel lands in a combat area with some Lesser Lycanthropes. Destroy them, and head to the end of the arena until you find a dead knight with a **Scroll** below the next Grip ledge. Use the Grip to lift yourself up to the top of the ledge.

Run along the narrow pathway heading to the left, and Grip Jump as soon as the floor collapses. If you fall to the ground below, just circle back and try it again.

LYCANTHROPE BATTLE

After jumping the gap, you stumble into a den of Lycanthropes. Take them out and walk toward the camera until you see a purple glow. Walk around a short wall to find the first **Crystal Shard**.

Second Crystal Shard

Walk away from the camera position to find the passageway in the back right corner of the area. Find the Grip Point above the dead end. Grapple to the top level. Walk toward the camera to find a dead knight holding a **Light Magic Gem**.

Head down the stairs on the opposite end of the ledge. Jump down into the crevice and battle the Lycans. Round the corner and use the Grip ledge on the decorative wall on your right to work your way over the large gap in the floor.

In the next dead end area, you find a Healing Font near the second **Crystal Shard** (purple glowing fire). Defeat the attacking Lycans, then claim the shard. Notice the glowing, half-buried gear wheel near the large gate in this area. This is a device that requires a Combat Cross upgrade. You'll have to come back here later to discover the secrets beyond the gate.

GATE WHEEL

Use the Stake upgrade on the Combat Cross (when you earn it) to crank the gate wheel. This action opens the gate, which uncovers the Dagger Upgrade from the Brotherhood Ark.

Return to the decorative wall at the gap you just crossed. Before crossing the gap, head to the top of the wall to find a destroyed room above. Inside, you can find a **Shadow Magic Gem** on a dead knight. You can also find a large belt of daggers in the adjacent room. Return to the climbing wall outside and cross back over the gap.

Remember, we still need three more crystal shards!

Third Crystal Shard

Head back around the corner and find the Grip ledge on the decorative wall. Jump up and hang onto the next ledge above the glowing one. The camera exposes a Grip Point high up on the same wall. Climb up the rope until your feet pass the dark row of bricks above the second Grip ledge. Swing out and jump and immediately latch onto the Grip Point on the adjacent wall behind you.

Climb up the rope to the second Grip Point, and then swing right to drop down and catch the Grip ledge on the short jutting wall corner below. Shimmy right along this wall, hand jump over a gap, and drop down onto a high walkway-like ledge. Be prepared to jump over a gap, as the pathway crumbles under your feet as soon as you move away from the Grip wall. Before you reach the next gap that you must leap over, another section drops out below your feet.

Turn left on the small ledge across the gap and leap out and latch onto a Grip ledge. Shimmy around the corner, jump to the Grip ledge behind you, shimmy right, and hand jump over a gap. Drop down to the slanted brick ramp (fallen wall piece) below you.

Greater Lycanthrope Battle

Follow the pathway down to an arena where you must battle three Greater Lycanthropes. The key to surviving this battle is to use your Light Magic to regain health and your Shadow Magic to inflict more damage. With some luck, you will have saved some energy from previous conflicts that you can use here. Take full advantage of the grab moves once you have the beasts stunned so you can finish them off with stakes and neck breaks.

Find the Grip ledge in the back right corner of the arena. Run across the ledge and leap over the hole. Use the Grip ledges in next corner to reach the top of the wall. Pull yourself up, and you'll be facing a waterfall fountain that spans an entire wall. Walk toward the camera on this ledge to find the third **Crystal Shard**.

Fourth Crystal Shard

Follow the same ledge away from the camera from the second Crystal Shard to enter a new area. Find a Health Font on the far end of the entry ledge to the new area.

Drop down to the ground level, and you'll find a glowing pillar blocking a passage. To the right of that, you'll find the fourth and last **Crystal Shard** in a corner. When you acquire the fourth Crystal Shard, you also acquire the Dark Crystal skill. With the Dark Crystal selected, press and hold the Secondary Weapon button to destroy it, releasing the demon contained inside. The energy within a complete Dark Crystal can be used to not only destroy powerful foes, but also to power ancient devices.

CAVE TROLL

A Cave Troll crawls out of a hole upon inspection of the large glowing obstacle. Beat the Troll until stunned and then mount it. Use the Troll to break down the obstacle in the next doorway, which creates a path to the beginning area.

Statues and Light

Now back in the beginning area where the Titan and Claudia wait, the statue in the center of the room is operational (as long as you have collected four Crystal Shards). Press the Use button while standing in front of the glowing statue. A light ray slices through the large stone door it's facing, allowing all three characters to enter the next room.

BROKEN CRYSTAL

If you broke the crystal before solving the door puzzle (if you used it to summon the demon from the Shadow Plane), you can gather three more pieces from the crystal spawn points distributed across the map.

Before you leave the area, take the fused crystal back from the slot in the statue. As the scroll hinted, you'll need it for other locks. Follow your team inside the next chamber.

You'll find another puzzle inside the structure. Place the fused Dark Crystal into the glowing statue in the back left corner of the large chamber. With the laser shooting out of the statue, grab onto the handle on the statue and turn it so the laser points at the statue directly across the room from it. Move to that next statue and turn the statue so the laser points to the third statue in the room. Now turn the third statue so the laser points at the next door. This opens the doors.

With the final door open, you can now continue toward the next level through the open doorway. You cannot take back the crystal from the statue.

LEVEL EIGHT:
SANCTUARY OF TITANS

The three companions enter the chamber of the Titans. What awaits them there is all that remains of the great technology of the Aghartians. This battle will test them all, and there is no going back now. The board is set, the pieces in play, and we shall see what occurs and who will emerge the victor. The child and her Golem will help, and I hope once the battle is won that Gabriel will have the courage to do what is necessary. Necessary for our quest to succeed, for there is still the matter of the Lords of Shadow, and their power is even more formidable.

Hidden Items
‡ 1 Shadow Magic Gem

Monsters
‡ Stone Idol Titan

Unlockable Trial
‡ Finish the level and defeat the Stone Idol Titan in less than two minutes

Boss Battle:

Stone Idol Titan

The Mage-Smiths were an order of Aghartian wizards who specialized in the creation of powerful artifacts. Most of their inventions were objects of common use, such as magical clothing or enchanted weapons and armor, but probably their most impressive creations were the Titans. These golems of gargantuan proportions were built for defensive purposes, but mages were forced to use them in the course of the war against the Dark Lords, during which most of them were destroyed.

Bring It to Its Knees

After the intro cutscene where the Titan reassembles itself, a fully functional Stone Idol Titan, which is the second colossus boss in the game, confronts you.

This enemy drops giant flaming boulders if you get too close. Also, being as massive as this boss is, it makes the ground shake with each of its steps, forcing you to jump to avoid being hit by the shockwave.

SHADOW MAGIC GEM

Find the **Shadow Magic Gem** on the dead Brotherhood knight lying up against a long rock on the left side of the arena.

The basic combat strategy is similar to the one used against the Ice Titan; you must climb onto its body to find and destroy the magic runes that animate it. However, in this battle, you start the ascension with a different method: you must first evade the Titan until it decides to throw a floating rock that surrounds its body.

When a rock is about to hit you, press the Use button to grab and throw it back to the enemy. You have to move the left stick counterclockwise in a rotary fashion to successfully complete the throw. This is the tricky part; you don't want to rotate the stick too quickly or too slowly. Try to match the speed indicated by the moving arrows around the onscreen left stick icon at the bottom of the screen once the rock is caught.

Once you manage to hit the colossus with the rock, it becomes momentarily stunned—it kneels down, allowing you to get aboard. You must use this time to get close to it and use the Grip Hook on its left leg to start the climbing challenge.

Climbing the Legs

The left leg must be Grip Hooked and grappled to. From there, you climb to the very top of the leg. To get to the very top, you have to shimmy to the inside of the leg (to the right near the top) and then shimmy back to the left once on the top rock layer. Once on the top edge, you must grapple to the right leg.

Once on the right leg, you must shimmy and ledge hang from section to section until you are on the outside of the leg. You must work your way down to the knee section to reach the first magic rune. Again, hold on tight when prompted and hit the magic runes ten times to destroy them.

Climbing the Arms

Once the right knee rune is destroyed, the Titan reaches for you. You can dodge to gain access to the swinging arm, but you will not be prompted to perform this tricky maneuver. To do this, drop down a few rock edge levels on the leg so that when it swings, the hand lands above you. When this happens, the swinging hand glows, indicating that it is ready for you to Grip Hook.

If you are knocked to the ground, you must throw another boulder back at the Titan and then grapple to the glowing left hand that pounds the ground after a successful boulder return.

Left Elbow Attack

Once on the left arm, climb to the elbow and hit the magic rune ten times to destroy it. While you are working your way up to this point, Claudia distracts the Titan to help keep you safe. As you did with the knee rune attack, as soon as you destroy the rune on the elbow, drop down a few levels so the next hand attack misses you and lands above your head. Grapple to the glowing right hand to continue the attack.

Right Elbow Attack

Once you've boarded the right arm, the Titan slams the ground and throws you off in a cinematic. The wrist glows again, so quickly grapple to it before it rises again. Climb the arm to the elbow and destroy the rune. As soon as it is destroyed, climb to the top of the elbow to avoid the other hand attack.

Head Rune Attack

After you have destroyed the right elbow rune, a distant floating rock glows soon after the left hand swings at you. Safely above this attack, grapple to that glowing rock and again to the forehead when the rock moves close enough to make the head Grip Point glow. Climb a little way up the head to smash the crown rune.

Dark Crystal Throw

After the tenth hit on the crown rune, Claudia tosses a Dark Crystal up to you during a cinematic. During this cinematic, you must press any button when the center ring glows in the halo around the Dark Crystal. If you miss, you must climb back up to the head and repeat until you get it right. If you get the button press right, the cinematic continues and you jam the crystal in the Titan's forehead, killing it instantly.

LEVEL NINE: THE BLACK KNIGHT

A great victory! Gabriel has won the trust of the girl, and together they wield a fearsome power. She is so young, so beautiful. Life is so fragile here on the edge of humanity, and yet in this unforgiving place she has managed to survive with the help of her Black Knight protector. Sleep will come and take them soon. Tired and exhausted, they rest, but this night, fate once again comes calling, and I fear my friend will never be the same again.

Relic

‡ Dark Gauntlet

Monsters

‡ Black Knight Golem

Unlockable Trial

‡ Finish the level and defeat the Black Knight Golem without using Light Magic energy

Boss Battle: Black Knight Golem

This Golem was created using similar techniques to those involved in the construction of the Titans. However, a human body was needed to imbue the armor with great power, so Claudia's father used the corpse of a mute killer and weaved his soul within the armor to forge this magical being. The Black Knight requires souls in order to function, so Claudia lures evil creatures so that he may devour them. Despite this, the Black Knight is not evil; the soul of the killer inside the armor hopes for redemption by protecting his ward, and sees a kindred spirit in the mute daughter of his creator, whom he has eventually grown to love.

Defeating the Black Knight

The Black Knight goes insane after finding Claudia dead, and recklessly attacks Gabriel. This enemy is very slow, but his attacks are extremely dangerous, so your best option in this combat is to use the dodge to avoid his sword as much as possible. Remember to switch the magic power from Light to Dark, to heal yourself when needed, and to inflict more damage with your own attacks.

Using jump attacks is also a very effective way of avoiding the boss's ground oil attack. If your feet enter the oil, you are temporarily stuck and cannot attack, block, or dodge. You are very susceptible to attack while stuck in the oil. To get free from the oil, repeatedly tap the button indicated on the screen.

JUMP THE SHOCKWAVE

A Dodge move won't be enough to evade the damage when the Dark Knight punches the ground; you must jump to escape the shockwave.

Once the knight suffers enough damage, he becomes temporarily dazed; he also becomes immune to damage, which is symbolized by his health bar turning gray. At this point, you have to use the Combat Chain on him to remove his armor. Press the Grab button while the Dark Knight is glowing to use the Combat Chain on him. When prompted, press the displayed button repeatedly. The first time you successfully complete this challenge, his armor is ripped off.

With no armor pieces left except for his helmet, the knight is almost done. The next time he is stunned, a successful Grip action causes Gabriel to jump on his back and struggle with the boss's helmet. Follow the onscreen button prompts to beat the challenge. If you beat the minigame, the Dark Knight finally goes down. Mask-less and defeated, the Dark Knight implodes, and the Dark Gauntlet becomes yours—now a permanent fixture on your arm.

CHAPTER III

LEVEL ONE: THE THREE TOWERS

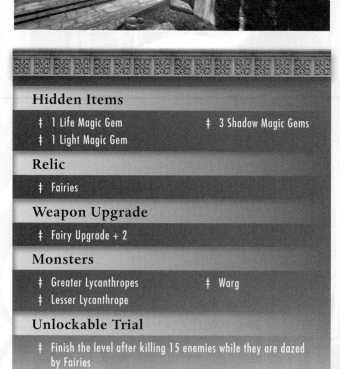

Dreams are a gateway to the mind, and now Gabriel has paid a terrible price for succumbing to his weariness. The many sleepless nights since his love was taken from him, the fear of falling into sleep, the nightmares that haunt him have all played their part. Did he murder this poor girl? Or is there some other explanation? Doubt gnaws at him now, eating his very soul. The Golem protected this child for centuries, loved her dearly, and there was no way he would have let Gabriel live, let alone give up the gauntlet. Few men could continue, most would abandon the quest, but something deep inside forces him ever onwards. A dark force has taken hold, and all creatures of the night will come to fear him now!

Hidden Items

‡ 1 Life Magic Gem   ‡ 3 Shadow Magic Gems

‡ 1 Light Magic Gem

Relic

‡ Fairies

Weapon Upgrade

‡ Fairy Upgrade + 2

Monsters

‡ Greater Lycanthropes   ‡ Warg

‡ Lesser Lycanthrope

Unlockable Trial

‡ Finish the level after killing 15 enemies while they are dazed by Fairies

Walkthrough

Dark Gauntlet

Gabriel continues his journey; he is getting closer to the first of the three Dark Lords. When you begin this level, the Travel Book opens to display information about your new appendage, the dark gauntlet. This piece of Aghartian mage-smith technology was not originally part of the design for the Black Knight Golem but was somehow magically melded with the construct during the final stages of its creation. Claudia's father included it because of the sheer power and the brute force that it gave the Golem. While he deemed it necessary in order to protect his beloved child, in truth, it has a much darker purpose.

Dark Gauntlet + Shadow Magic

Approach the glowing statue at the start of the level and press and hold the Block button and the Direct Attack button together to charge up the attack and then release the buttons to issue a massive punch that knocks the statue a few yards in front of you.

CHARGED PUNCH

Tip: When using the Gauntlet Punch, the time that the button is pressed determines the strength of the attack. Hold the button to maximize the punch and move the statue completely with one hit.

The statue smashes into a gate, causing the wall to crumble a bit in the right corner. This reveals a Grip ledge that you can use to get over the wall. However, the gate is unbroken. To break down the gate, you need to combine Shadow Magic with the gauntlet.

If you need energy to do this, hop the wall, fight the Lycans, and then find the Neutral Elemental fountain in the adjacent courtyard found by heading toward the camera from the front gate. Fill up on energy and then climb back into the original area using a Grip ledge in the back left dark corner of the Elemental fountain courtyard.

Break the Gate

Now full of elemental energy, enable Shadow Magic so you are glowing fire red, and then use the Gauntlet Punch to hit the statue through the front gate. The statue is hit so hard that it continues through the gate and toward the edge of the chasm. Defeat the attacking Lycans.

You can use the Grip Point in the statue to jump to the other side. If you don't see the Grip Point on the end of the statue, then it's not all the way to the edge of the chasm on the rails. Hit it again to make sure it is all the way to the edge, then use Hook Tip to grapple to the next landmass across the chasm.

To the City Entrance

Continue through the ruins and pass under the arch. Walk toward the camera to find a Dark Crystal deposit.

Jump to the next earthen platform to find a dead knight's **Scroll**. This Scroll merely speaks of the knight's vague discoveries of this land.

From the back right edge of this land pillar, make a series of jumps to the right over multiple smaller pillars. The last pillar before the larger landmass has two access points. You can land on top of the pillar and spot a Brotherhood Ark on the next ledge (you cannot reach this until you have a particular upgrade), or you can latch onto a lower ledge and work your way around below the surface and then use Grip Points to reach the next landmass.

DEMON FROM THE SHADOW PLANE

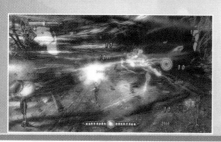

If you found the Dark Crystal deposit in the beginning of the level, then you have a full Dark Crystal. Try using it to summon the Demon from the Shadow Plane during this battle to wipe out all the enemies. This is a quick way to complete the battle.

Twinkle, Twinkle Little Fairy

After all the Lycanthropes are defeated, the fairies give Gabriel his new relic: the **Fairy Blossom Container**. After that, they fly towards the ancient city door and fuse with the carvings in the stone, opening the door in the process. The receptacle given is used to safely store magic fairy blossoms. When used, the fairies sprout and attack any nearby enemies until the villains are stunned.

FRAGILE FAIRIES

The fairies are very fragile. When you use them, they consume their own health, exploding after awhile with a display of green magic dust.

Before you enter the temple, find the dead knight **Scroll** on the right side of the courtyard. In it, the knight describes a dream he had where he encountered the Queen of the Fairies, and with that he died a satisfied soul.

The Temple of Lycanthropes

Inside the inner temple of the Lycanthropes, find the Neutral Elemental fountain on the right near the first set of incomplete stairs. Further ahead, you find a glowing dead knight on the floor almost directly below a glowing broken beam jutting out of the top of some obstructed stairs. The dead knight holds a **Shadow Magic Gem**.

Use the Spiked Chain to grab the glowing beam and repeatedly press the indicated button to rip the beam down, creating a few Grip ledges to reach the exit above.

Use the Grip Point outside to swing across the next gap to reach the wide ledge where a dead knight lies. He is carrying a **Light Magic Gem**. Return to the tower and enter the next area.

In the middle of the courtyard, look for a bull statue. As you've done before (the last time you've seen one of these), pull the horn and turn the bull in a clockwise direction to lower the twin gates on the building showing in the background. Enter that tower now.

A new glowing locked door is seen in the back of the tower. An onscreen message says that you need to find three fairies to open this door. Defeat the attacking Lycans and then exit the tower heading through the left exit.

Beat down the Warg in the next tower and then stun him and mount him. Ride the beast back through the previous tower, and now take the right exit. Pass through an exterior walkway and enter another tower. Inside this tower, take the left exit to reach a decrepit covered passageway.

Second Floor (Vine Climb)

Use the Warg to climb the glowing vine at the end of the passageway. On the next level, you can find an exit on the left and right and a third one straight ahead forward. The exit on the left contains a Healing Font. The exit on the right has a vase with daggers and a dead knight with a **Shadow Magic Gem** (come back here after completing your current task with the Warg). Head through the far exit to reach a broken bridge.

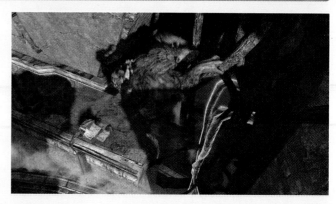

Use the Warg to jump the gap and then to destroy the Greater Lycanthropes on the other side. Once the battle is over, strangle and dismount the Warg.

A device in this combat area opens the doorway inside, but you must to deal with all the enemies before trying to open it, or they will attack you and interrupt the process. Approach the device and press the Use button. Press any button again when the center halo ring lights. Gabriel then begins cranking the wheel to open the nearby gate.

Inside the tower, there are two possible exits (left and right); the left exit takes you directly to the first fairy, while the right requires you to solve the magic puzzle in the room and then travel through the right exit, eventually recovering the second fairy that way. It's best to leave the puzzle in this room unsolved right now and just use the Grip Point above the left exit to travel to the first fairy.

The First Fairy

First, move to the left exit (the balcony overlooking the city below). Use the Grip Point above the exit to swing out of the tower. While you're swinging, the camera angle changes, and you can spot another Grip Point at the top of the tower face.

When Gabriel is in the highest point of his swing, press the Grip button again to use the chain on the higher Grip Point, which takes you to a climbing area along the broken tower "face." This leads to the tower top, where you find the first fairy.

After retrieving the fairy, walk toward the camera to find the Neutral Elemental fountain. Refill your energy on this, and then find the dead knight Scroll to the right of this fountain. This scroll solves the puzzle in the tower you just left (blue, red, red). Good find! To return inside the tower you just left, use the Grip ledge and Grip Point on the edge of the tower rooftop near the Neutral Elemental fountain and the dead knight with the scroll.

The Second Fairy

From the top of the tower where you retrieved the first fairy, continue forward, toward the camera. Don't forget to fully recharge both magic energy gauges before continuing, as you must use those powers soon. Behind the neutral magic fountain, a Grip Point allows you to grapple back to the floor below.

The path that leads to the second fairy is locked behind a puzzle that must be solved in order to continue: there are three stone symbols engraved in stone in the wall. With a magic power active, Gabriel can use the symbols to charge them with magic. However, the symbols can only be charged with one particular magic type; an incorrect guess will be only a waste of energy, while discharging any charged symbol.

The answer to the puzzle is found in the knight Scroll found on the rooftop near the elemental fountain. The tip: blue, red, red. So, use Light Magic on the leftmost symbol and then use Shadow Magic on the remaining two symbols to solve the puzzle. When the puzzle symbols are correctly charged, the camera shows a giant device moving over the main building (out the right exit).

Now, head through the right exit to find a high Grip Point exposed on the statue that was repositioned from solving the magic symbol puzzle. Swing from the three Grip Points on the three peaks of the statue. The third Grip Point allows you access to a balcony on another tower.

Enter the doorway on the balcony of the second floor of the right tower. Inside, you'll find two identical devices, one inside the room and the other in the bridge that connects this tower and the next one. But as you quickly discover, there is only one handle to use them both. Find this handle through the left exit at the bridge gate. Pick up the handle and approach the glowing gear device there on the bridge. A Greater Lycanthrope attempts to make this a more difficult challenge. Defeat the Lycan, then pick up the handle again.

Use the handle on the glowing mechanism on the bridge. Press any button when the middle halo glows. This happens a few times. This lowers the gate on the bridge. Take the handle out of the device and move back into the tower, and repeat this procedure on the mechanism inside.

Once this device has been used, the gate on the right side of the bridge opens, and the device in the tower opens the gate near that mechanism. Head back out the left exit to the end of the bridge and use the Grip Point beyond the lowered gate on the next tower. Move around to the backside of the tower to find another high Grip Point.

Grapple to the top and jump to the ledge to the left. Shimmy along the Grip ledge heading left across a gap and then pull up to a platform where you'll have to climb a few more Grip ledges and use one more Grip Point grapple maneuver to reach the top of the tower. The second fairy is on the top of this tower.

Walk toward the camera and find the lower ledge on the top of this tower. Keep heading toward the camera to the outside edge to find a dead knight with a **Life Magic Gem**.

The Third Fairy

Find the glowing ledge on the edge of the tower to the right of the fairy stone. Drop down a couple ledges and use the Grip Point to grapple down the tower. Along the way, you'll spot a room in the tower through a broken wall to the left. Use the nearby Grip ledge to shimmy to the opening and jump into this room. On the floor, you see a dead knight holding a **Shadow Magic Gem**. Return to the outside wall of the tower and continue your descent into the tower below. You'll soon recognize your position in this earlier tower.

Return to the magic symbol puzzle tower and enter the exterior balcony through the gate that was opened using the handle found on the bridge. Use the Grip ledges on the wall on the right side of the exterior doorway. Climb up the outside wall as high as you can, hand jumping right over an obstruction and continuing upward until you must shimmy around a corner beam and continue to the top of the tower—no Grip Points for grappling needed. Find the third fairy on top of this tower.

Return To Fairy Puzzle Door

Return to the central tower on the second floor where you found a Shadow Magic Gem. Use the Grip Point above the hole in the floor of this tower to drop down to the lower floor (some minor ledge gripping is necessary, as well). Enter the next courtyard where the bull lever device is located and defeat the attacking Greater Lycanthropes. Defeating them with a Dark Crystal makes the fight easier, and each drops a whole Dark Crystal when they die.

Fairies in Battle

If you consider using your newly found fairies in this battle, be warned that they are very fragile, and you may have to return to the same tower rooftop ponds to replenish your supply.

The Greater Lycanthropes break the bull lever, so now you must find another way inside to the fairy door. Head to the right side of the tower, and you'll find a Grip point on the side of the wall. Use the Spiked Chain to pull the stone out of the wall (follow the button prompts to successfully do this), creating a small structural avalanche that reveals a few beams that allow you to Grip jump up to the small window above.

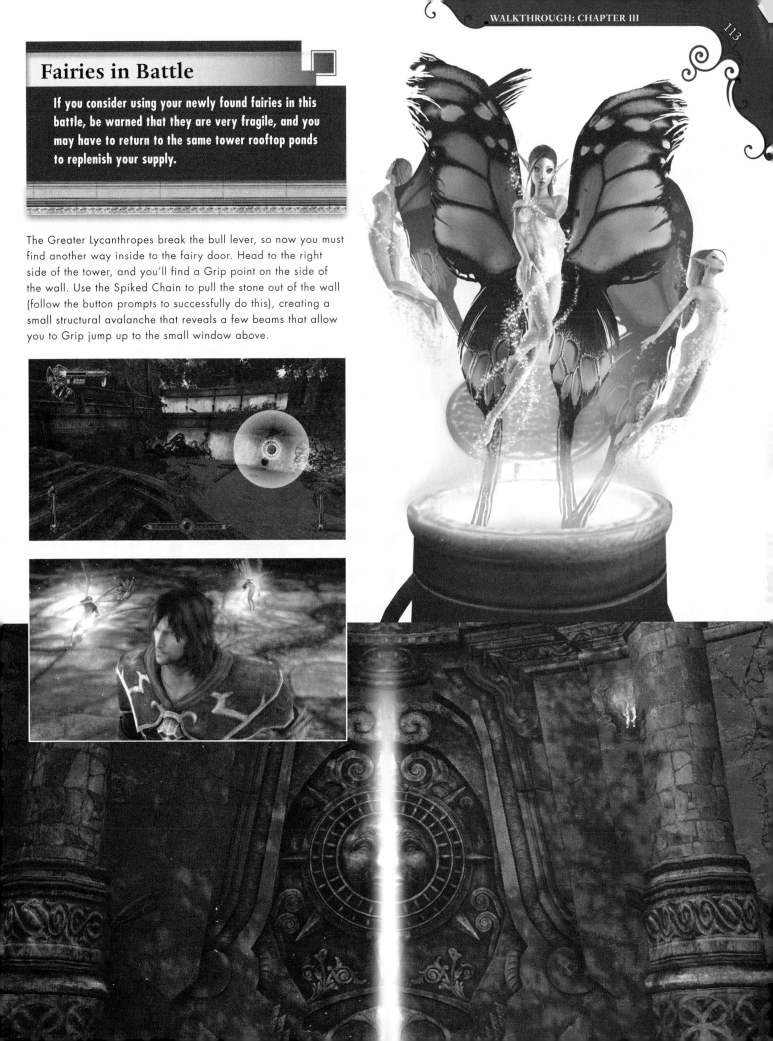

LEVEL TWO:
THE DARK LORD OF THE LYCANTHTROPES

Monsters

‡ Lycanthrope Dark Lord

Relics

‡ Cyclone Boots

Unlockable Trial

‡ Finish the level and defeat the Dark Lord without using Light Magic energy

Gabriel has fought long and hard to get to this point, and now he faces his stiffest challenge. The Dark Lord of the Lycans must be defeated if Gabriel stands any chance of bringing his beloved back. I fear he will suffer more than he knows once he discovers the truth, and yet his hatred and burning desire for revenge cannot be underestimated. He has the gauntlet and he has Gandolfi's weapon. He is a force that even the Dark Lord will struggle to deal with. Good...soon he will overcome this evil. Soon the world will be free of the Lords of Shadow and plans long dreamt of will come to fruition. Go, my friend...go and break this creature once and for all.

Hammer Power

The Dark Lord can use his evil magic to empower the hammer. When he uses this ability, the weapon glows with lighting energy. His attacks in this state are more dangerous, so try to avoid them.

TROUBLE IN FAIRY-DISE

Fairies have no effect on bosses.

Boss Battle:
Lycanthrope
Dark Lord

To defeat Cornell, dodge often while being particularly dutiful about jumping over his ground pounding shockwave attack. Use your quickest, most damaging blows, but save your Dark Crystal for the second phase of this battle. Fighting with Shadow Magic enabled causes significantly more damage than using the same attacks without it. This first stage of the boss fight should prove to be surprisingly easy, which should also scare you a bit.

After you've knocked all the health out of the boss, a checkpoint is reached and a cinematic plays. In this movie, the boss looks defeated at first, but then buries his hammer into the middle of the arena and transforms into his next form...

Phase 2: Lycanthrope Dark Lord

When the Dark Lord seems to be defeated, he channels the power of the moon to transform into a monstrous giant Lycanthrope, bigger even than the Greater Lycans. He still uses the Cyclone Boots' power, but this time he uses it to make quick dashes and charges against you.

Using your Shadow Magic now will not have as much effect on the boss as it did in the first stage. However, now is a good time to use the Dark Crystal to summon the Demon from the Shadow Plane. This takes about a quarter of the boss's health.

When you knock the boss's health down to about 5%, he then concentrates his powers in the eight stone monoliths surrounding the area. This transfers the Dark Lord's life force to the monoliths. From this moment on, the Dark Lord is immune to damage. The boss's health bar turns gray, representing the health "stored" in the monoliths. Now you must destroy the monoliths to damage the Dark Lord.

Once the eight monoliths are shattered, the Dark Lord is all but defeated; only a quick minigame more, and you will be able to claim his power. There are a series of halo ring challenges to complete the multi-leveled melee attack on the Dark Lord.

It begins by a successful pull on the Spiked Chain to yank the creature onto its back. This is followed by a second similar move to again yank the boss back to the ground with the chain.

When the Dark Lord begins floating up in the air in the blue rays in the middle of the stage, you must again press any button as the center halo is lit to pull the boss back down to the ground.

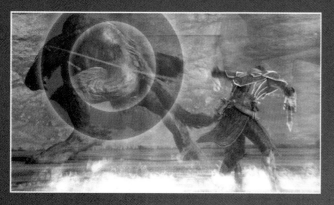

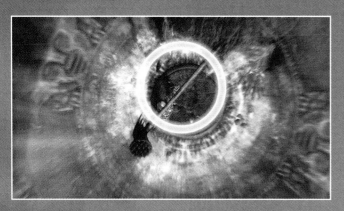

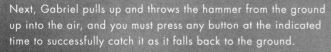

Next, Gabriel pulls up and throws the hammer from the ground up into the air, and you must press any button at the indicated time to successfully catch it as it falls back to the ground.

Next, you must successfully swing the hammer at the Dark Lord.

Finally, you must successfully jam the broken hammer handle through the boss's mouth and force it through the back of his head. That completes the boss fight.

After the cutscene, you earn a new relic to use in your journey: the Cyclone Boots. These allow faster running, and with them, you can also perform powerful shoulder charges.

To exit the arena, you have to make use of your new relic. Only a Cyclone Boot sprint jump can get you out of there. To sprint, just double tap the left stick in the direction you want to run. Leap to the exit hallway and then use the Grip ledges in the back to reach the high ledge, where you meet an interesting character that will "fly" you to a faraway destination.

SPRINT

The sprint ability granted by the boots is not unlimited. Get used to the distance that you can run using them before trying to jump out of this arena.

CHAPTER IV

LEVEL ONE: MOUNTAIN FORTRESS

The deed is done. Cornell is no more. Such a pity that the brotherhood of light, the order to which we both belong, should also be the reason why the world is in such chaos. Gabriel, you have proven your worth, my friend. You have a piece of the God mask. It is said this relic can bring back the dead. It is said this relic can bestow power beyond any man's reckoning. Now with the help of the old God, he heads toward the land of the vampires and further into the heart of darkness.

You may think I am helping you, but you would be wrong. I serve no one. You would do well to remember that!

Hidden Items

‡ 1 Life Magic Gem
‡ 2 Light Magic Gems
‡ 1 Shadow Magic Gem

Weapon Upgrade

‡ Fairy Upgrade +2

Monsters

‡ Chupacabras
‡ Ogre
‡ Cave Troll
‡ Small Troll

Unlockable Trial

‡ Finish the level and defeat the Ogre without being hit by his attacks

Walkthrough

Mountain Trail

After being dropped off on a mountain trail by a giant eagle that swears that it's not doing you any favors, follow the trail across a shallow waterfall stream and then fill up your magic energy using the Neutral Elemental fountain just before the narrow mountain pass.

Just through the narrow mountain pass, you'll find a dead knight on the ground just before the path bends to the right and heads to the entrance to a mountain fortress. The knight's Scroll speaks of an Ogre in the castle and mentions that having something that makes you run faster would help when confronting the monster.

Approach the locked doors of the fortress at the end of the mountain trail. You stand before the abandoned fortress that serves as lair for the Crow Witch. Now with the Cyclone Boots, you can perform a Shoulder Dash attack, which allows you to break through some obstacles. Activate Shadow Magic, then press and hold the Block button to charge the attack. Once charged, push the left stick in the direction you want to break through obstacles. In this case, it would be forward, and you'll be splintering through the doors. Return to the previous Elemental fountain and refill your gauges before advancing through the outpost.

Head through the covered hallway and turn right when you reach the fork in the path. Around the corner, you'll find a dead knight holding onto a **Life Magic Gem**.

The Broken Bridge

Turn back and head left at the previous fork, and you'll come to a deteriorating section of the tower, which seems like a dead end. Walk off the edge and latch onto the Grip ledge. Work your way around the curved exterior wall to reach the continuing pathway on the other side of the tower.

Battle the Trolls on the pathway. These Trolls are cannon fodder and shouldn't be a match for Gabriel, especially after you buy some of the new available combos. Once the enemy is eliminated, use sprint while running along the left side of the covered path and then jump over the gap to reach the next side. You must jump over the smallest section of the gap, located along the left edge.

Path to the Fortress Entrance

Once you reach the other side of the broken bridge, another small group of Trolls ambushes you.

DESTRUCTIBLE WALL

Look for a secret breakable wall across the broken bridge. The wall houses another Brotherhood knight with a **Shadow Magic Gem**. To get to it, use a Shoulder Dash movement against the wall to demolish it.

Back on the path to the fortress, you soon find a new obstacle: the gap can be crossed like the previous one, using the sprint. Remember to double tap the left stick to start the sprint and jump almost at the edge of the platform to clear the gap.

GRIP POINT GRAPPLE VERSUS SPRINT JUMP

You can also try to use the Grip Point movement to cross the gap: use the chain grip on the glowing point on top of the mountain and move sideways while being suspended; you can jump in the direction that you are moving here.

There is a secret zone, accessible through the Grip Point in the mountainside above the first gap. After using the Hook Tip in the Grip Point, climb to the top of the chain, and you'll discover a ledge you can grip onto with your hands. Moving to the right here reveals a new Grip Point, placed higher on the mountain. Climb the chain up to the top ledge. Here, you'll find a Dark Crystal deposit and a dead Brotherhood knight carrying a **Light Magic Gem**.

Continue towards the fortress entrance. Along the way, you'll come across another gap to sprint jump across. The fortress's main entrance is blocked. Find the dead knight **Scroll** at the top of the steps before the blocked entrance. You can climb the mountain to the left using the Grip Points in two areas during your ascension. The second grapple takes you to a ledge full of Trolls.

The Ogre's First Appearance

While dealing with the small Trolls, the first boss makes his appearance as he ominously moves into position behind the wall. The humongous Ogre starts punching the wall, trying to bring down the entire platform. After some hits, the leftmost section of the platform falls down, along with anything standing over it. Be sure to stay around the right edge of the platform to avoid falling with it.

The next Ogre hit clears the path to the continuing platform. Use the Grip Point to swing across the gap to reach the ledge on the other side of the tower. The Ogre keeps smashing the wall from the other side, eventually bringing down the original platform altogether.

The Ogre's Hand

As soon as you reach the new platform, the Ogre furiously launches a punch at the wall, breaking it. This allows him to get his arm out through a hole. Now the Ogre tries to catch you and squeeze you to death. This is also the first chance given to inflict some damage on the boss.

The Ogre touches the platform, looking for a chance to grab you. After a few seconds, it punches the ground and moves its hand forward to reach out and grab you. If it does grab you, then you can repeatedly press the indicated button to stay alive and inflict some attacks on the Ogre that not only cause some damage but also causes the Ogre to release its grip on you.

COMPLETION TRIAL HELP

Use magic! Use the Shoulder Charge to quickly get away from the hand before it has time to catch you. This keeps you from getting hit and helps with the completion trial. Additionally, use the Shadow Magic to reduce the hand's health in just a few hits.

Some well-placed attacks force the Ogre to retract its arm. This happens when the boss's health bar is reduced to zero. This gives you time to reach the end of the platform before he recovers. Use the high Grip Points to grapple over the moat to the next platform. If you fail the second grip, the Ogre recovers, catching you and forcing you to replay the previous combat.

After crossing the moat, the full Ogre is seen for the first time. Notice the Neutral Elemental fountain over the short gap on the far left side of the bridge. You can replenish Light and Shadow Magic energy by standing close to the fountain—the gap does not hinder the process.

The Ogre slams the platform, trying to hit you. You must unload your attacks on the hand when it hits the bridge, hitting it as much as possible before it retracts to launch another punch. The Ogre's attacks are unblockable, so dodging is necessary.

SHOULDER CHARGE DODGE

It is easier to avoid the Ogre's attack using the Shoulder Charge. Perform a Dodge Roll with Shadow Magic enabled.

GRAB HIM

When the health bar of a special boss monster turns gray, it means that normal attacks won't damage him, and you have to find another way of causing harm. Most times, it must be done with a Grip move.

The Ogre's anger increases when close to half of its health is depleted. At this point, its health meter turns a solid gray, indicating normal attack invincibility. A special attack is also released: a fist slam that releases a shockwave on impact. The camera zooms in while the Ogre screams, forewarning of the hit. To avoid the wave, you must jump when it smashes the ground. If done correctly, the Ogre's hand starts glowing, allowing you to use the Spiked Chain on it.

In a quick cutscene, the Ogre raises the hand, pulling up off the ground with it. Be ready to mash any button when the center halo ring lights. With correct timing, you attack the Ogre, hitting it in the right eye before the monster has any time to react. The Ogre is now blind in the right eye.

Blind in One Eye...

The combat continues now with the Ogre completely enraged and blind in one eye. The Ogre grabs a section of the platform and uses it to increase the damage of his fist-pounding attack. Each hit made with the boulder releases a shockwave, forcing you to jump over it before attacking the hand.

After dealing some damage to the Ogre, the beast drops the boulder and begins repeating the attack from the first phase of the battle. Again, the glowing hand urges you to use the Spiked Chain. This time, you spring into the air after grappling the glowing hand and then have to press a button when the middle halo glows when centered on the Ogre's left hand. This is followed by a quick halo challenge around the Ogre's head. Done successfully, the Ogre's left eye is gouged out, leaving him completely blind.

Finishing Move

During the final phase of combat, the Ogre's health bar is all but empty and gray, so your normal attacks won't inflict damage. The monster is blind and now sniffs the air to find you by scent. You have to dodge three of the Ogre's quick, downward clenched-fist punches. After which, the Ogre billows up and lets out a mighty growl, leaning its head forward for emphasis. The Ogre's head now glows, allowing you to grab it with the Spiked Chain.

MIDDLE OF THE ROAD

So that you aren't wasting your efforts during this phase, stand in the middle of the bridge so that the monster's head hangs over the pointy stone pillar when it screams. The pointy pillar is the device that actually kills the beast.

The Spiked Chain latches onto the boss's tongue. You must successfully hit any button when the center halo glows around the beast's head. Done correctly, Gabriel yanks the Ogre's head down once. The beast pulls back, and you must repeat the pull challenge. This tug-of-war happens three times in a row before Gabriel successfully impales the Ogre's neck on the sharp pillar stone.

Inside the Fortress

With the Ogre dead, you can abandon the platform by sprint jumping from the right end of the battle platform, across a large gap and into the fortress through a broken wall.

Follow the pathway until you drop down into a large hole in the floor. Here, you'll find a Brotherhood knight holding a **Scroll**. Walk away from the camera and jump out of the hole to reach the continuing pathway. You'll find a secret area behind a statue at the end of this hallway.

SECRET STATUE

After sprint-jumping into the fortress, follow the path and find the statue in the wall at the end of the hallway with the dead knight Scroll in the hole. You have to push the statue using the Gauntlet power (hold the Dodge button and press the Direct attack button while facing the statue). In the hidden area, you can find a fairy, and another dead Brotherhood knight with a **Light Magic Gem**.

Follow the path left at the secret statue. You'll reach another area featuring a locked gate and one of those glowing gears. You must come back here once you've upgraded your Combat Cross.

STAKE UPGRADE SECRET ROOM

Once you've acquired the Stake upgrade for the Combat Cross, return to the wheel here to crank open the adjacent gate. Complete the halo ring challenge to crank open the gate. **Fairy Upgrade +2** is inside this secret room.

Taking a left at the fork (where the right path leads to the Stake Upgrade Secret Room) leads to a dead end. Look for the Grip ledge on the right. Use that to reach a small ledge to stand on. Once there, you can find a high Grip Point that lets you grapple over the rubble-blocked Doorway. When you land in the next area, a horde of Small Trolls immediately attacks you.

Cave Troll Rider

This time, the Small Trolls attack with greater numbers, but won't pose too much of a threat; use them to recover magic energy if needed.

When the first Small Troll wave is eliminated, a Cave Troll appears through the round grate in the middle of the arena. Small Trolls won't stop appearing at this time, either.

To exit the arena, you must ride on a Cave Troll and use it to smash down the metal door at the farthest side of the arena. So once you've mounted the Troll, destroy the Small Trolls and then start punching the glowing gate until it is destroyed. The new area reveals the fortress tower.

The Chupacabras

TOWER BASE

Continue through the gate towards the witch tower. At the top of the stone stairs awaits a new enemy: a Chupacabras. In a short cutscene, this grotesque creature steals your relics and powers and then disappears in a puff of black smoke.

You can continue forward, but you find the tower entrance blocked by a wooden door. To cross it, you need to recover the relics' powers from the Chupacabras. The monster has fled toward the exit on the left at the bottom of the stairs. Head back down the steps and take a left into the narrow nook and climb the ledges to pass under a tall arch doorway.

There's a very large hole in the floor in the next area. Travel across the boards on the left to reach the Neutral Elemental fountain, which is useless to you now that the monster stole your relics. Just beyond the energy fountain is a column you can climb that allows you to jump backwards onto the adjacent scaffold.

Climb the scaffold and use the high Grip Point to grapple and drop onto a beam (catching yourself by hanging by your hands). You'll see the Chupacabras on the ledge below your feet. Drop down to that ledge.

When you finally find the Chupacabras, a simple grab is enough to get all the relic powers back.

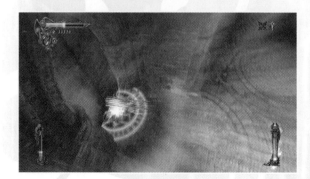

Fill up on energy using the Neutral Elemental fountain and then once again, return to the stairs where you first found the Chupacabras at the tower base. Approach the massive doors. You must Shoulder Charge on the door to break it, completing the level as you pass through the broken door.

LEVEL TWO: THE CROW WITCH

It is a sad tale of the witch who guards this fortress. A sad tale of love lost. A tale not so dissimilar to our brave hero. Yet pity is not something he can feel anymore. He is blind to it. The pity of these so-called "evil" creatures will be laid aside for revenge. And so goodbye, once beautiful Malphas, you will trouble mankind no more, and when you are gone into the void, know that love destroyed you in the end.

Hidden Items

‡ 1 Life Magic Gem

‡ 1 Light Magic Gem

‡ 1 Shadow Magic Gem

Weapon Upgrade

‡ Holy Water Upgrade +2

Monsters

‡ Swordmaster

‡ Small Troll

‡ Crow Witch Malphas

‡ Witch Child

Unlockable Trial

‡ Finish the level and defeat the Crow Witch without killing more than two of her sons

Walkthrough

Witch Tower

FIRST FLOOR

Gabriel finally reaches the inside of the witch tower. Find the dead knight **Scroll** near the locked door below the bird's head. The Scroll leaves a clue to how to get into the tower. The door is locked, and the door at the top of the stairs behind the bird's head is blocked, so the only way upwards is climbing the exterior wall.

Find another dead knight on the stairs near the blocked doorway. This knight holds a **Light Magic Gem**. Head through the tall, narrow exit on the left staircase to reach the snow-covered mountainside outside.

Secret Small Troll Cave

Once outside, there is a secret path that leads to a Small Troll cave below. Do not Grip climb up the right ledges yet; instead, from the first ledge, jump to the platform below. The camera shows another ledge further to the left. Take the leap to that lower ledge and then hang off the edge using the Grip ledge. A glowing Grip point becomes visible further to the right. Use it to reach a small cave beneath the tower.

Inside the cave, you find some Small Trolls and the corpse of a fallen knight, carrying a **Shadow Magic Gem**. Defeat the Trolls and refill your energy using the Neutral Elemental fountain found near the front of the cave (head toward the camera to find it). The path in the cave leads back inside the tower. You can break the door from this side, using a Shoulder Charge.

EXPERIENCE POINT FARM

Every time you find a spot like this Small Troll cave, with countless enemies and a Neutral Magic fountain, it is a perfect opportunity to earn some experience points. Also, remember to fully refill both magic meters after smashing though the door to continue the level completely recharged.

Go outside again, and this time, climb the mountain ledges to your right. A Grip Point becomes visible from this point, allowing you to rappel and climb upwards, getting to a big stone gargoyle on the wall. Grip again to the top and climb until you reach the stained-glass window. This is your entrance to the second floor of the tower; just kick the wall twice (push any Attack button while in rappel stance), take momentum, and watch how Gabriel shatters the window and breaks into the tower.

Swordmaster Battle

SECOND AND THIRD FLOORS

In the second floor of the tower, you fight your first Swordmaster. These are souls of slain warriors who didn't leave the material plane and remain trapped. Their sole mission is to torment living beings. Once you have beaten down one to a certain degree, you can use the Spiked Chain on them to grab them and run them through to finish them off. Two more of these Swordmasters appear after you defeat the first.

These enemies move very fast and can counterattack some of your skills. When fighting more than one, stay alert and keep an eye on the enemy with the lighting charged sword, as he is the most dangerous of them.

After you've destroyed the three enemies, the witch opens the path to the next floor, sending some of her crows to break through the door blocking the way up. Follow the stairs to encounter a Grip Point grapple that takes you up to the next floor.

Three Swordmasters

Three more Swordmasters appear on this level. This time, you face all three of them at the same time.

DARK CRYSTAL?

If you still have a full Dark Crystal, this can be a good time to use it, as it is able to destroy all the enemies in a single blow. Fairies (with or without the Light Magic power active) can also help you manage the enemy attacks, thus having a much easier time of this battle.

When all the Swordmasters are dead, the camera reveals the Grip Point that'll take you on route to the top floor balcony. Climb the chain from the first Grip Point and jump to the Grip ledge to the right. Use the chain on the next Grip Point over the next arch, and then climb that chain all the way to the top to latch onto the ledge to the right. Shimmy to the broken railing to reach the balcony.

Before you exit the tower, head to the left along the top balcony. Find the Health Font at the end of the path. Follow the balcony around to the exit and refill your energy on the Neutral Elemental fountain on the balcony. Notice the dead Brotherhood knight lying next to the fountain. He holds a **Life Magic Gem**.

Climb the wall to the left of the balcony exit. Continue climbing and shimmying around corners, scaffold, and nooks until you reach the top gargoyle. From here, you can jump onto the top of the tower roof (no Grip Point chain grapples here). The climb shouldn't be a problem; just look for the path before moving and don't jump unless you see Gabriel looking for a potential climbable ledge.

Boss Battle:
The Crow Witch

Phase One

As soon as you set one foot on the tower rooftop, the Crow Witch makes her grand appearance. The first thing she does is throws three eggs at you. If they hit the ground, they immediately release her Witch Children on impact. Try not to get hit by the eggs, as they inflict heavy damage. During this first phase, you should be able to throw at least one of the eggs back at her by grabbing it with the Spike Chain and following the onscreen left stick rotation. Hitting her with her own egg causes her major damage.

After throwing her eggs, the witch starts flying in circles around the tower, stopping every once in a while to attack you. One of her attacks is a sonic wave that can stun Gabriel, leaving him defenseless against her children. When you see her screaming, watch out for the circular distortion area in the ground—it is not too difficult to dodge or jump over the shockwave, but it can surprise you if the attacking children distract you. For this reason, concentrate on taking out the Witch Children first and foremost. If you do get stuck in the sonic wave, repeatedly press the button indicated on the screen to break free.

Another of the witch's attacks is the crow swarms. When she is about to launch one of these attacks, you'll see her children covering, and the camera focuses on her. When she stops, all the crows following her rapidly fly towards you. This attack cannot be blocked. To dodge them, pay attention to the swarm timing, and use a lateral dodge to avoid it.

The only moment that the witch is vulnerable is when she stops in midair to summon more of her children; you need to exploit that action in order to damage the witch, by returning the eggs to her in midair. After some attacks, her health bar turns gray again, and her body glows. At this point, use a Grip action when close to her to jump onto her head. The witch starts flying away. In the following minigame, you force her to crash into the tower, remaining stunned for some time after.

During the cutscene, press the displayed button as fast as you can to ram her into the ground.

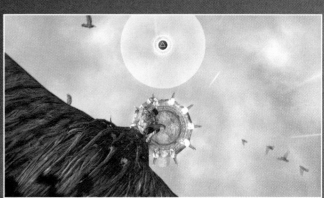

Phase Two

After riding the Crow Witch into the ground after a successful minigame moment, the witch lies helpless on the edge of the battle arena. The remaining enemies try to block your way to the witch, giving her time to recover. Ignore them, and head on directly against the boss. Now she can be attacked with normal attacks

If you can attack her enough in this round, a new Grip Point allows you to use the chain on her again; successfully completing the head removal minigame finishes her. This minigame consists of nothing more than repeatedly pressing the indicated single button. Destroying the Crow Witch also quickly reduces the fortress tower to a pile of rubble.

Fortunately for Gabriel, Pan comes once again to his rescue, saving him from certain death. After the final cutscene, the level ends successfully.

CHAPTER V

LEVEL ONE: VEROS WOODS

So it seems Pan has saved Gabriel once more; his arrival is most fortuitous! Gabriel now enters the outskirts of the vampire's territory. A cold winter has gripped this land for centuries, driving out the inhabitants to warmer climes. Those stubborn enough to stay have contended with the cold death that visits them each and every night, taking their loved ones away forever. The vampires thrive in the cold and terrorize the living who crave warmth and companionship. This night, a warrior will come. A knight in shining armor with death at his side. He comes for you. Creatures of the night!

Hidden Items

‡ 2 Life Magic Gems   ‡ 1 Shadow Magic Gem

Monsters

‡ Chupacabras   ‡ Warthog
‡ Goblin   ‡ Small Troll

Unlockable Trial

‡ Finish the level recovering your relics from the Chupacabras in less than three minutes since stolen

Walkthrough

Return of the Chupacabras

The escape from the Crow Witch Tower ends in a frozen, labyrinthic forest. The pathway splits in multiple branches, some of them leading to rewards and others ending in combat zones.

Defeat the Goblins at the first fork and then take the pathway to the left at the first fork to find a Fairy Blossom. You could use these fairies later on Head back to the fork and take the right pathway to find a Shoulder Charge destructible wall in a short path on the right (easily seen from the main route).

Behind this first breakable wall, you find a Dark Crystal deposit that partially fills your crystal meter. There's also a nearby dead Brotherhood knight with a **Life Magic Gem**.

As soon as you enter an open clearing along the main route, a Chupacabras appears and steals the relics from you. Without the relics' powers, you won't be able to exit the forest, so you must find the Chupacabras and force it to return them.

LISTEN UP!

To find the sneaky Chupacabras, sometimes you have to pay close attention to your surroundings and listen closely for the little monster's voice. It tells you how close to it you are.

Stolen Relics

The Chupacabras left you relic-less and powerless in a zone inhabited by mountain Goblins. This variety is fiercer and tougher than the other Goblins you've previously encountered, so try not to lose much time fighting them. Your best bet is to run directly for the Chupacabras to get your relics back. You'll have more opportunities to vanquish the Goblins later.

There is a path on the left in the Goblin camp, but ignore it for now. The Chupacabras has teleported to another exit, the one at the back of the area. Run out of the camp using the right pathway. As soon as you get close, the monster vanishes again, disappearing in a cloud of black smoke.

Just a few yards from where you saw the Chupacabras disappear outside the Goblin camp is a crossroad where three paths fork from the main road. Take the center path, and soon you reach the Chupacabras, which disappears again.

Second Goblin Encampment

The center pathway leads directly to a small Goblin encampment, where a bunch of these pesky creatures attack you. A Warthog accompanies them.

SECONDARY WEAPONS

Without the relics, you cannot use the Light Magic to recover health. However, you still have secondary weapons. Using the fairies gathered earlier to stop some of the enemies from attacking is a smart tactic, but be careful not to use them all; you'll need them again soon.

Beat the Warthog down and mount it. You must ride on the Warthog to break the Goblin encampment door down. After mounting, just run towards the gate to charge against it.

With the door destroyed, you can eliminate any remaining Goblins and move forward. The Chupacabras appears a few meters away through the broken door and then teleports to a ledge above.

This same location features a Health Font and a dead Brotherhood knight. Dismount and defeat the Warthog, replenish lost health, and grab the **Scroll** from the knight. The Scroll hints at using fairies to distract the Chupacabras.

To reach the Chupacabras on the ledge, climb the wooden scaffolding starting with the Grip ledge above the dead Brotherhood knight. Shimmy around the corner and pull up to the top of the ledge. Now just jump to the right over the gap, toward the Chupacabras' hideout. The Chupacabras will zap you off the ledge.

The key is to take heed the knight's message in the Scroll. Release some fairies to distract the little monster, and then jump to his ledge. Pull up to the cave entrance and grab the Chupacabras while it is glowing and distracted. Now you get your relics back.

Chupacabras' Cave

Look inside the Chupacabras' cave. There's a dead Brotherhood knight with a **Scroll** inside. The Scroll speaks of Dark Crystals, an old man, and the mysterious relics. Now that you have your relics back, head to the back of the cave and take advantage of the Neutral Elemental Fountain to fill up your magic meters.

Grabbing Goodies before You Leave

Before leaving the forest, why don't you explore it again? With the relic powers back (especially the Dash), you can discover more than one secret area around the level. Return to the three-way fork just beyond the first Goblin camp.

Taking the leftmost road away from the camp places you at a breakable stone wall. Use Shoulder Dash to break the wall and find a **Life Magic Gem** on a dead knight along with a Dark Crystal deposit.

Head back to the three-way fork and take the middle or rightmost pathway and just keep heading left at the next fork. You'll reach another Shoulder Dash wall. Beyond this one, you find another Dark Crystal deposit and a dead knight with a **Shadow Magic Gem**.

Path to the Village

Either head beyond the Chupacabras cave and drop down onto a lower path to reach the continuing path, or head back to the first Goblin camp and take the left path within the camp. You'll reach a Shoulder Dash breakable wall near a Neutral Elemental Fountain.

After a new encounter with a few Goblins, you'll drop down to a wider path, which is blocked by large stones. This is also the left fork in the first Goblin camp. Use the dash (with the Dark Magic power active, press Block and then move the left stick in any direction) to break through the stones. If you don't have enough Dark Magic, you can go back and get some from defeated Goblins.

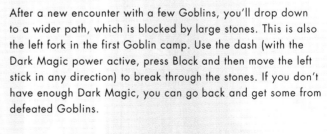

Just through the broken wall lies a dead knight near a column of stones on the right side of the road. He holds a **Scroll**. The knight writes about being close to Wygol and Vampire Castle. From there on, enjoy the view of the Vampire Castle as you run along the snowy path towards the isolated village.

LEVEL TWO: WYGOL VILLAGE

This village is one of the last vestiges of human civilization left in this place of death and cold. It lies not far from the Vampire's Castle, our next objective. I have some matters to attend to here, matters that could spoil our plans. I will deal with them and try to rendezvous with Gabriel later. He has not slept in days, not since the girl. The pain is etched on his face still, but in his soul only hatred drives him. We will not speak of it. He must not know I have seen everything, that I have followed him this far.

Hidden Items

‡ 1 Shadow Magic Gem

Weapon Upgrade

‡ Ghoul

Relic

‡ Stake

Monsters

‡ Ghoul

Unlockable Trial

‡ Finish the level without allowing Zobek to kill a single Ghoul

Walkthrough

The Village

In the beginning of the level, you find yourself in a dark alley leading to the village's main throughway. There is a secret in the first building on your right, but since you don't have Seraph Shoulders yet, you'll need to come back when you do.

WINGED CHALLENGE

When you have both Shoulder Dash and Seraph Shoulders, you can break through the wall at the top of the stairs on the first building on the right in the village (located at the beginning of the level). Shoulder Dash through the exterior wall and then use the wings while in the back corner of the room to reach a ledge with a Brotherhood Arch on it. Open the arch to earn the Holy Water Flask Upgrade + 2.

Encounter with Zobek

Soon after entering the village, you find Zobek praying over a body in the cemetery. He informs you that the vampires ravaged the village after hearing that you killed the Dark Lord of Lycanthropes. You can't help but feel a little guilty for the village's loss. These people's only hope lies in an old abbey, not far from here, but the mad abbot who lives there won't give up the relic so easily.

Graveyard Battle

After the cutscene, you find yourself in a graveyard, accompanied by Zobek. Soon, a new type of enemy attacks you: Ghouls. These enemies can vomit poisonous goo and feed on corpses to regain health.

After killing a Ghoul, don't move too far from its corpse; other Ghouls try to devour it to recover their life, so it's best to wait around and guard it until the Ghoul corpse disappears.

The Ghouls emerge from holes in the ground found in various areas around the graveyard. The first one is on your right as you begin the challenge, the area where the Ghoul in the cutscene came from. Fortunately, a large statue, which seems pretty unstable, stands next to the hole. With the help of Zobek, you can knock the statue down over the hole, obstructing the Ghouls there.

DROPPING THE FIRST STATUE

Use the Spiked Chain to grab the glowing statue near the Ghoul hole. Press the Area Attack button to call Zobek to help push. Press repeatedly on the Direct Attack button indicated on the screen to pull the statue at the same time that Zobek pushes it. Look for a final button press (Area Attack) indicator on the top of the screen to finally topple the statue over the hole. Some Ghouls may escape during this last stage, but the toppling statue usually squishes these blood bags.

DROPPING THE SECOND STATUE

Immediately after you neutralize the first Ghoul hole, more Ghouls start spawning from another hole to the left. This time, the statue is not close enough to the active Ghoul hole to push it in. You have to get behind the statue and push it using the Gauntlet punch. Then, repeat the same minigame used during the first statue topple to knock this one in the active Ghoul hole.

DROPPING THE THIRD STATUE

Find the dead Brotherhood knight with the **Shadow Magic Gem** in the back right corner on a pile of rubble.

The final fissure tears up the ground at the back of the cemetery, and more Ghouls emerge from it. By this time, you know what to do, but this time you cannot get behind the statue blocking the entrance to the crypt near the hole. Find the breakable wall around the left corner of the crypt entrance. Use Shoulder Dash to break into the crypt. Refill your energy on the Neutral Elemental Fountain in the back corner. Use Shadow Magic with Gauntlet Punches to move the statue to the hole.

After that, repeat the previous steps to topple the statue into the final Ghoul hole. The third statue partially falls over the graveyard's exit gate, allowing you to fully open it with a Shoulder Dash to get to the mausoleum in the next yard.

The Relic in the Mausoleum

Fill your health meter using the Health Font on the left side of the mausoleum entry stairs. To the right of the entry stairs, you come across a dead Brotherhood Knight. His Scroll explains that Light Magic is the only thing that can dispel the Ghouls' poisonous vomit. Once inside the mausoleum, you discover it seems to have no exit.

Step up to the altar and receive your new Combat Cross upgrade: **Stake**. The artisan who made the chain and Hook Tip for the Combat Cross wanted to give the weapon even more options for hand-to-hand combat, especially against supernatural creatures of the night, and so he designed the Stake attachment that eventually gave the Combat Cross the nickname of "Vampire Killer."

With the Stake Cross in your hands, the strange gear machine glows on the left wall, hinting a possible interaction with it: press the Use button while close to it to start the challenge. You must stick the gear and crank it four times by pressing any button when the center halo glows. This opens the exit near the mechanism. Enter that doorway to end the level.

LEVEL THREE:
ABBEY CATACOMBS

We delve deep below the abbey ready to face the evil confronting us. The abbot, Vincent Dorin, was once a good and kindly man who helped the people of Wygol, but now he has become a devious coward who has holed himself up in the abbey and rigged it with traps of cunning. The people, unprotected, have paid a heavy price for his treachery. Night has fallen outside, and we will be open to vampire attack at any time. We must be on our guard. We must work together, if we are to succeed in acquiring the relic that the abbot guards. This will help us greatly in defeating the vampire horde later.

Hidden Items

‡ 1 Life Magic Gem   ‡ 1 Light Magic Gem

Monsters

‡ Ghoul   ‡ Vampire Warrior

Unlockable Trial

‡ Finish the level without allowing Zobek to fall a single time during combat

Walkthrough

 ## When Vampires Attack

Gabriel and Zobek are together in the catacombs that connect the village graveyard and the abbey. Shortly after they enter the area, vampires attack. The vampires appear in waves. To open the exit at the far end of the room, you must figure out the mechanism in the middle of the room while fending off the vampires.

Find the handle that operates the door mechanism in the middle of the room. Place that handle in the mechanism and then turn it to slowly open the exit. As soon as you release it, the mechanism resets, so Zobek's help is needed. What he will do is hold the mechanism (thus the gate) for enough time to let you cross under the gate before it closes.

Rotate the mechanism using the left stick. When the device reaches its furthest push point, press the displayed button to call Zobek for help. The trick is to make sure that you defeat all the vampires before trying to open the gate, or any hit received causes you or Zobek to release the handle, which drops the gate instantly.

Now you can cross the open door and reach the adjacent chamber, but something must be done for Zobek, who is still fighting vampires in the first area. Lucky for him, you can push a statue in the second chamber to break a hole through the metal gate—using the Shadow Magic plus Gauntlet Punch. If you don't use Shadow Magic, the punch will not be hard enough. You must use these combined powers a few times to get the stone close enough and then through the gate.

Return to the original chamber and help Zobek defeat the final wave of Vampire Warriors. Once Zobek and Gabriel are safely reunited again, replenish your energy using the Neutral Elemental Fountain in the second chamber and then continue towards the abbey. The large door at the back is closed and locked; you need two keys to open it.

First Abbey Cloister Keys

Both keys can be accessed by heading through the metal gates found on either side of the second chamber. To open the doors, you use two door mechanisms like those you found in the first chamber. Each one is connected to the nearest locked door; they only lack the handle needed to be able to manipulate them.

Head back to the first device in the first chamber and take the handle out of it. Open the right door first. There is a small passageway with a deadly trap that activates as soon as you enter.

The ceiling starts falling down over you and Zobek, but luckily for you, Zobek stops it over his head. At the same time, he urges for you to do the same with the next one, which has started to fall.

COLLAPSING CEILING

Move as fast as you can towards the next ceiling slab using the left stick. As soon as you start to hold it, repeatedly press the Direct Attack button until prompted to press the Area Attack button to tell Zobek to advance to the next block. The whole sequence repeats twice.

After escaping trap, look for the **Cloister Key** in a nearby candlelit nook. Just grab it and head back through the previous hallway (gears pull the ceiling back into place, making it safe to travel through) to the previous door chamber.

Second Abbey Cloister Keys

You can find the second key by getting through the left door. Grabbing the handle from the previous device and using it on the mechanism near the left door helps you begin this quest. Once you've opened the door, take the handle out of the door mechanism and bring it with you into the new area.

When you enter the large chasm, the last key can be spotted in the center of the gap on a currently inaccessible pillar. To reach it, use the handle on the mechanism on the far end of the entry platform. Call Zobek over to hold the device in position while you get on the cart that was moved to the end of the platform when you cranked the device to the furthest position.

Jump on the platform, and Zobek then moves it to the opposite ledge. Follow the ledge to the center pillar and claim the Cloister Key. Now head back to the previous ledge and follow the path toward the camera to find a step bridge where you can find a dead Brotherhood knight with a **Life Magic Gem.**

Continue heading to the left on this bridge, and you'll find you can drop off the edge to reach the original ledge at the entrance. Head back to the door chamber with the final key. To open the locked door, place both keys in the slots on either side of it. Follow the large stairwell up to the inner cloister.

The Abbey's Inner Cloister

Inside the abbey, you and Zobek must deal with another of the abbot's puzzles: some kind of teleportation wall stands in one of the cloister corridors. When you cross through it, you are magically transported back to the glowing seal near the entrance.

Your objective is to get to the door that leads to the library, but this magic teleporter sends you elsewhere before you can reach it. In the center of the cloister, you can use a strange piece of machinery to manipulate the portal system.

Like other similar devices found in the same level, this one is missing a fundamental piece: the metal bar used to spin the mechanism. You can find it nearby, in the passageway that borders the cloister. More precisely, find the dead Brotherhood Knight in the middle of the courtyard. He's holding a puzzle hint type of **Scroll**. Enter the passageway entrance that this knight's head and spear are pointing toward.

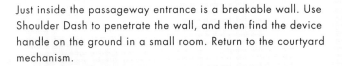

Just inside the passageway entrance is a breakable wall. Use Shoulder Dash to penetrate the wall, and then find the device handle on the ground in a small room. Return to the courtyard mechanism.

Insert the handle into the device. Now that the mechanism is complete again, you can use it to modify the position of the magic seal that marks the teleport destination: as you rotate the device, the camera points to the seal, showing you the location that you will get to after crossing through the magic teleporter wall.

Possible teleport destinations

PUZZLE SOLVED!

 ## Puzzle Solved!

To solve the puzzle, you have to spin the mechanism's arrow until it points to **Location #4**, which is 270º from its initial position.

You need Zobek's help to beat the puzzle: he needs to grab the handle after you get the device in the desired position and then hold it for the time that it takes you to quickly get to the teleport wall and jump through it.

LIGHT MAGIC GEM

One of the teleport destinations (**Location #2**) seems to lead nowhere, but instead allows you to enter a hidden room with a dead Brotherhood knight holding a **Light Magic Gem**. Once you have the prize, climb the wooden wall to the right of the knight and hand jump through the hole in the top of the gate wall to drop down into Ghoul battle. Defeat the Ghouls and return to the courtyard mechanism.

HEALTH FONT AND KNIGHT SCROLL

Point the device at **Location #3** to find a Health Font and a knight with a **Scroll**. The Scroll speaks of the dead knight's anguish. Use the Spike on the Combat Cross on the gate gear to leave the small cell.

LEVEL FOUR: ABBEY LIBRARY

The traps laid by the abbot have proved tricky, and yet we have managed to break into the inner cloisters and the library is close at hand, if memory serves. My friend looks weary and troubled. The weight of the world on his shoulders. I can see he is holding a terrible secret deep within. He is trying to bury it, and in its place the anger is taking over. We must not delay. We must find Dorin and take what we need before we are dragged down with the guilt. The need of the many outweighs those of the few now. We can shed no tears for those lost, we must be strong and we must destroy the Lords of Shadow at any cost.

Hidden Items

‡ 2 Light Magic Gems ‡ 1 Shadow Magic Gem

Monsters

‡ Animated Armor ‡ Gremlin

Unlockable Trial

‡ Finish the level and beat the mirror and lights puzzle in less than 2:30 minutes

Library Corridors

You and Zobek are now free to enter the library. Follow the rightmost corridors to the end to find a dead knight holding a **Light Magic Gem**.

The Library

Enter the doorway along the left wall, and you'll enter the abbey library where a cutscene plays. Zobek moves forward, and after looking around for a second, hints at the existence of a secret entrance to the abbey tower where the abbot hides. At the same time, some pieces of armor fuse together to form a new enemy: Animated Armor.

Animated Armor

Zobek is trapped behind an iron gate and this time asks for your help. You must protect him while he inspects the library shelves, looking for a secret entrance. You must defeat two Animated Armors. They don't take much damage until you remove their shields. To do this, beat on them until they raise their shields in front of them. The shield will glow when it is time to try to remove it. Use the Spiked Chain to grab onto the shield, and then repeatedly press the indicated button to pull the shield away. With the shield gone, your normal attacks now inflict more damage.

Be sure to jump into the air to avoid the Animated Armor's ground pounding shockwave attack.

When the enemy's body glows (which happens with around a quarter health remaining), press the Use button to jump onto the enemy and pull at its chest armor. Complete the halo ring challenge to successfully pull the chest plate open. Then, press the indicated button repeatedly to jam the Combat Cross inside the chest and unhinge the life that is animating the ghostly armor. This is a finishing move. The enemy is eliminated after this move, if done correctly.

SOMERSAULT ATTACK

A very useful movement against the Animated Armors is the Somersault: hold Block and then press the Jump button to leap over the closest enemy. Then strike from its back, where the armor is most vulnerable.

Finish the two Animated Armors, and Zobek will find what he was looking for in the next cutscene. Zobek finds and pulls a lever that opens a secret exit in the ceiling on your side of the locked gate. You leave the room through this secret passage using your Hook Tip while Zobek hangs back to defend the entrance.

Puzzle of Light and Mirrors

The abbot had a good idea to defend against the vampires: a set of doors that can only be opened using the power of sunlight via mirrors mounted on statues to redirect the light beams.

The library is divided into three zones. In all of them, the objective is to redirect the light ray toward a door with a sun symbol. It is a puzzle similar to the one found in the Stone Idol mausoleum. Find the hint Scroll on the body of the dead knight found at your feet the moment you enter the attic, where the first light and mirror puzzle is located.

AREA PUZZLE ONE

Fill up on the Neutral Elemental Fountain in the first area. There is only a mirror statue in the room, so push it to the light beam using the Gauntlet Punch and then rotate it so the beam bounces on the mirror toward the door in the back of the room with the glowing dot on it. Find the dead knight on the floor in the books to the left of the light source window. He holds a **Scroll**. It's a tip instructing you to use fairies on the enemies here.

AREA PUZZLE TWO

Initially, the second puzzle area seems identical to the first one, until you realize that there is no reflector statue in the second room and the beam is stopping on the bookshelf, which cannot be moved.

Enter the third room. Gauntlet Punch the statue near the bookshelf into the path of the beam. Turn it so it shines diagonally to the wall of the first room (refer to the picture).Exit the third room out the rightmost door (adjacent to the mirror you just moved). This next room is a book depository. Head to the end of the hallway and turn left to find a dead Brotherhood knight with a **Life Magic Gem**.

Now head back and continue down the right pathway (the only remaining untraveled route). This leads to another mirror. Use Gauntlet Punch on it to move into the doorway at the back of the same hallway. Head back to the mirror you moved prior to this one in the third room. If it isn't aimed up properly already, turn it so that it hits that last mirror you just moved into the doorway. This opens a door to the stairwell behind the bookshelf in the same room. Head upstairs.

ZONE 3

The last zone is the hardest. Now upstairs, defeat the flying Gremlins and then move around the balcony corner until you reach the closest statue. Gauntlet Punch it once toward the balcony rail and then again toward the light beam.

Rotate this mirror until the beam hits the second statue a few meters away. Make sure to enter the small gazebo at the bottom of the short set of steps behind this mirror statue. Break the stuff on the floor to uncover a dead Brotherhood knight on the floor. He holds a **Shadow Magic Gem**.

Now the ray must be redirected to the other side of the room. Head to the second mirror statue and stand on the left side of it and Gauntlet Punch it into the direction of the light beam being thrown at it.

Push this second statue along its own path until it reaches the end of its rail. Turn the mirror so that the beam is reflected across the gap and through a small hole in the opposite wall.

Follow the ray to the other side of the room, where you find a new mirror statue. Gauntlet Punch this mirror statue to the next room at the corner in its rail system. Just get it out of the way of the current light beam direction for now. Use a Shoulder Dash on the breakable wall the beam is currently targeting. If you need energy, you can find a Neutral Elemental Fountain in the previous large hall.

Defeat the Animated Armor in the newly revealed room, then Gauntlet Punch the mirror statue in this room into the path of the light beam passing through the hole you put in the wall. Now turn the mirror so the light is bounced onto the small wooden door in the back of the room.

Replenish your energy and then Shoulder Dash through this wooden door. Now the way is all clear; all you have left to do is to push the statue that sits on the rails behind this broken door to the end of the rails (closest to the broken door), and then turn it to face the last door at the end of the same hallway. Enter the now open door to end the level.

Level Five: Abbey Tower

The tower at the Abbey of Wygol was once a place where men of God sought knowledge and protected the people with Christ's love. Now it is the refuge of a man driven insane by fear. Dorin has abandoned his people to death or worse. A powerful relic keeps the vampires at bay, and we must take it if we stand any chance against the Dark Lord's minions. I know of a secret way that will take me to the top of the tower by a different path. Gabriel will have to find his own way for now.

Hidden Items	
‡ 2 Life Magic Gems	
Relic	
‡ Holy Water Flasks	
Monsters	
‡ Ghoul	‡ Gremlin
Unlockable Trial	
‡ Finish the level after finding and destroying 100 breakable objects before the allotted time runs out	

Walkthrough

Fortified Tower

After beating the puzzle of light and mirrors, you stand in another cloistered area; the fortified tower of the Abbey is the last obstacle in your way to get the relic that the abbot keeps to defend against the vampires.

The tower is surrounded by a moat filled with deadly wooden spikes; a fall here would be fatal. Leave the tunnel and enter the moat pathway. To the left of your exit, you find a dead Brotherhood knight with a **Scroll**. The Scroll speaks of Dorin's traps and his hidden relic.

To the right out of the original hallway, you have a run-in with Gremlins and Ghouls. Take them out with extreme prejudice.

Head to the end of the right pathway to find a broken area in the short wall that allows you to access a covered brick passage. Walk toward the camera first to find a dead Brotherhood knight with a **Life Magic Gem**.

Now move away from the camera and follow this passage to another area that looks like the exterior area you just left. Find a **Scroll** on a knight lying beside a dead tree. This Scroll is a great tip on receiving Neutral Elemental Orbs. Defeat the Ghouls and Gremlins in this area.

Sprint jump across the gap in the pathway here, and you'll reach the tower entrance. The camera shows a wooden bridge at the other side of the moat; it is raised right now, but you can pull from its top with the combat chain until it collapses. Press Grab while the bridge is glowing to use the chain on it. When prompted, press the displayed button repeatedly.

Cross the boards into the tower entrance and defeat the Gremlins. After dealing with all of them, you can safely start the climbing area. First, use the Combat Cross Spike on the gate wheel to pass. Follow the stairs around to the climbing wall.

DEFEATING FLYING CREATURES

The best way to deal with a flying enemy such as the Gremlin is to usually wait for it to get close to you, and then grab it (pressing the Use button).

While climbing, watch out for unstable ledges, and try to jump from them as quickly as possible. The falling debris can also throw you down while grappling; jump backwards to avoid this.

Once you reach the first rooftop, continue forward, where you'll find another building to overcome. You must dash and jump to reach the ledge of this building. Around the first corner, you can find a ledge with a dead knight holding a **Life Magic Gem**. Return around the previous corner and continue shimmying right to follow along the climbing path, jumping back and forth from wall to wall in this narrow alley.

When you reach the top of the second tower, grapple through the boarded window to enter the building. Inside, you'll meet up with Zobek again.

In the ending cinematic, you find the abbot, Dorin, and the relic he hoards to himself. You take it and exit the tower, leaving the abbot in an unprotected state. The Vampire Warriors claim another victim—holy or not. On the way out of the tower, a wounded boy points you in the direction of a village in need of help. Zobek stays behind to assist the child.

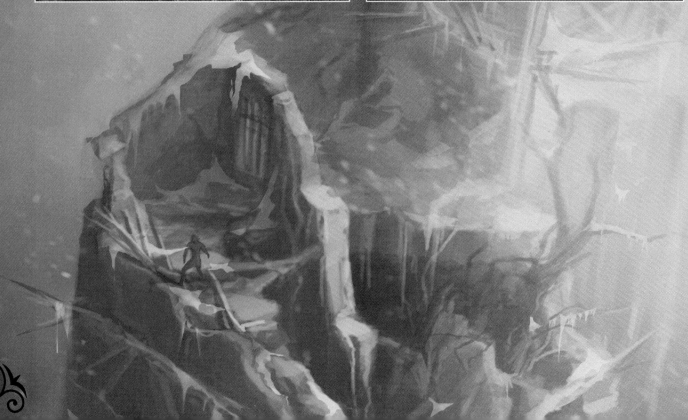

LEVEL SIX:
BRAUNER

The power to defeat the vampires is now in our hands, and that bastard Dorin has no doubt met his maker. If anyone deserved death, it is he. No one will shed a tear for his miserable life. Countless others have met the same fate by his hand. The quest is going well, we have what we need to confront the Dark Lord and I sense Gabriel's determination to see this through. The vampires must know we have the relic, and I am sure they will move to stop us, if they can.

Monsters

- ‡ Lieutenant Brauner
- ‡ Vampire Warrior

Unlockable Trial

- ‡ Finish the level after attacking the Elite Vampire four consecutive times with its own blade

Boss Battle:
Lieutenant Brauner

Now you find yourself back in the village besieged by vampires in a full-scale attack. In the initial alley where you begin this level, refill your magic with the Neutral Elemental Fountain and replenish lost health using the Health Font. Use the Grip Point above the flaming crates blocking the entrance to the village.

HOLY WATER RELIC

Gabriel took a relic from the abbot, which is especially destructive against vampires: Holy Water Flasks. These can affect most enemies, but vampires suffer more damage from them than others. You can also use them with the Light Magic power enabled to create a protective shield around you, which reduces incoming damage.

A few waves of Vampire Warriors attack you when you enter the main street of the village. Use Holy Water on them to really soften them up; they'll love it. Use grabs as much as possible to finish off the vampires quickly. After annihilating the Vampire Warriors, the big daddy shows up to the fight.

Lieutenant Brauner, the Elite Vampire, is a powerful enemy who uses mostly melee attacks. He also carries a long throwing blade, and he can transform into a group of bats to move quickly around the arena.

LONG THROWING BLADE

When the boss uses his blade for the first time, the camera shows you a close-up of the weapon as it flies toward you. If you press the Grab button while it is in mid-air, you return it back toward the enemy, inflicting heavy damage.

You have to lower the boss's health until you stun him. This happens when his health drops by half. The beginning of this stage occurs when you knock him to the ground. As soon as he gets up, he is stunned, swaying and glowing. Approach him and press the Use button to begin the minigame where the end result has you ripping his wings off with your bare hands. This is done in two halo ring challenge moves.

Continue the battle and stun him a second time. This is usually possible when he has about 10% of his health remaining. Again, he will fall and then stand up and glow while swaying. Approach him and press the Use button to begin the finishing move minigame.

The first halo ring challenge has you smacking his jowls with the Combat Cross. The second halo challenge is blocked even if completed correctly. Then, a struggle occurs. Press the indicated button repeatedly until a cinematic shows you break free and quickly steal the boss's long throwing blade from his back. Next, you slash the boss's arm off and then slice him down the middle. You finish him with the Combat Cross's Stake through the heart.

LEVEL SEVEN:
CASTLE SEWERS

Wygot village is safe, for now. The vampires have lost one of
their commanders, Brauner, and news will travel back to the
Dark Lord quickly. This is a blow, but it won't take long for
them to regroup. Luckily, one of the villagers has revealed to
us a secret path into the demon's castle. This will lead Gabriel
into the sewers and then up into the very jaws of death. The
villagers called him "God Savior," and his weapon they called
"Vampire Killer." Ah, Gandolfi, how that would make you
smile. As for me, once my business here is done, I shall follow
my friend and aid him where I can.

Hidden Items

‡ 1 Shadow Magic Gem

Monster

‡ Skeleton Warrior

Unlockable Trial

‡ Finish the level after killing three Skeleton Warriors without
  destroying their shields

Walkthrough

Pipe Mania

Following the indications of the remaining villagers,
Gabriel is going to enter the Vampire Castle through
the old sewer system. A cave in the mountainside leads
to the sewers. You can find a Health Font as soon as you enter
the sewers. Refill your life energy before moving forward.

Soon, you notice that a stream of sewer water flowing through a
pipe in the wall blocks the continuing interior path; don't try to
cross it, or it'll push you into the muddy waters below, which are
infested with Naiads. Instead, use the lever on the wall before
the water stream to stop the flow from a few pipes temporarily.

NEUTRAL ELEMENTAL FOUNTAIN

Continue past the first water hazard to find a Neutral Elemental Fountain in the next corner. This fountain, although handy, is what makes it difficult to complete this first task, because while you are refilling energy, you are not moving quickly enough to get past the second water hazard and into the next area over the bridge.

As fast as you can, sprint all the way past the first pipe, the Neutral Elemental Fountain, and then the second water pipe (double tap the left stick to sprint) on the bridge. There is another mechanism between the position of the two pipes, but don't bother with that now; just concentrate on getting to the other side before the water flows again.

Use the Combat Cross Stake on the glowing gear on the left side of the new room. While turning the gear in a cinematic, a new type of enemy shows its bony face. This is a Skeleton Warrior.

Skeleton Warrior Battle

The most noteworthy feature of the Skeleton Warrior is that the first time they are defeated, they can reconstruct themselves and be made ready to continue fighting. To avoid this power, use a ground attack such as the Gauntlet Punch against their bones to completely destroy them.

Once you deal with all the skeletons, use the device found in the arena again. It opens one of the gates of the sewers. Once done, head back to the bridge and use the lever there to open the gate just below.

Jump down into the first muddy sewer and find the dead knight **Scroll** at the bottom of the first set of stairs. There is a slight tip at the end of this document concerning the very frustrating gate trap you are about to encounter.

Before you pass though the opened bridge gate, head to the back right corner of the area to find an island in the poison and mud with another dead knight. This knight holds a **Shadow Magic Gem**.

Now head through the opened gate into the second mud and poison area. Cross to the opposite platform. Before you pass into the next area, stop at the doorway and head to the island in the corner toward the camera (front left corner of the room). Here, you can find a dead Brotherhood Knight with a **Scroll**. This one features a tip about taking out Skeleton Warriors's bones so they don't reanimate. Now head into the next hallway to beat the floor spike puzzle.

Sharp and Pointy

Even though the castle is centuries old, some of its traps still work. Only a tricky corridor stands between you and the exit. At one end is a metal gate that slams shut on approach, and at the other end is the mechanism that opens the gate. The mechanism on your side of the hallway is a large button embedded in the wall. It can only be activated with a powerful hit (the Gauntlet Punch should be used; press and hold the Block button and then press the Direct Attack button).

As you move toward the metal grate on the floor, the trap activates, and dozens of metal spikes emerge from holes, instantly killing anyone standing over them. Your first thought would be to punch the button and sprint towards the open gate; only, the gate slams shut when you leave the spike grate.

SPIKED FLOOR PUZZLE SOLUTION

The answer is in the silver daggers; charge them with Shadow Magic to give them enough power to activate the button from a distance. Just stand next to the closed exit gate and throw the Shadow Magic charged dagger at the button down the hall across the spiked floor. The door opens, giving you more than enough time to exit the trap.

Once through the gate, simply use the single Grip Point at the top of the chasm to grapple out of the level.

CHAPTER VI

LEVEL ONE: CASTLE COURTYARD

Despite his best efforts to try entering the castle unnoticed, the vampires know that Gabriel is coming. Night is fast approaching, and soon he will have to use all his wits and powers to defeat what nightmares inhabit this place of death and decay. His strength grows by the day, and yet his anger intensifies deep within. He eats little and sleeps less. She is there in his thoughts, his beloved Marie, he knows that his journey is far from over. This castle I fear will push him into the abyss from which there is no escape.

Hidden Items

‡ 1 Life Magic Gem

Monsters

‡ Animated Armor
‡ Skeleton Warrior
‡ Vampire Warrior
‡ Warg

Unlockable Trial

‡ Finish the level and kill three Skeleton Warriors while you are mounted on a Warg

Walkthrough

Descent to the Castle Dungeons

The Vampire Castle finally stands before you. To get out of the chasm, climb across the middle beam and climb up the opposite wall until a Grip Point is seen near the top. Grapple climb to the top. With your feet on the ground again, you face the castle's main entrance.

As you enter the courtyard, the camera shows a magnificent view of the front of the castle. You can find a bag of daggers by sprint jumping across a large gap near the locked entrance to the maze garden.

To continue forward, you must climb the tower on the left side of the courtyard (next to the Health Font) to shimmy and jump over the left edge of the gate that separates this courtyard from the next.

Animated Armor Battle

In the ground in the center of the second courtyard, there is a metal grate that you can open using the nearby Stake mechanism. This is the entrance to the castle dungeons, your next destination. As you start to manipulate the Stake mechanism (or if you get too close to the castle door), two Animated Armors materialize in the courtyard and attack you.

It's nearly impossible to fully open the grate with the enemies attacking, so defeat both of them before continuing. Once done, you can safely open the grate on the ground and jump to the darkness below. You have a narrow window of opportunity to jump into the hole before the grate closes again, so be quick after opening it.

Castle Dungeons

You are now in the castle dungeons. The vampires keep savage beasts like Wargs and Trolls in cages here, ready to be drained of blood. Walk toward the camera and use the Neutral Elemental Fountain at the beginning of the path.

In this area, a couple Skeleton Warriors rise from the ground and attack you. While you are occupied with the Skeletons, the vampires open one of the cells, releasing a Warg; as you have done before, you must mount it. Sometime during the battle, go get the knight **Scroll** from the dead knight in the far back left corner of the hallway. It speaks of the Wargs and Troll captives.

LIFE MAGIC GEM

The first cell on the left side of the hallway (nearest to the Neutral Elemental Fountain) can be broken using a Shoulder Dash. Inside the cell is a dead Brotherhood knight holding a Life Magic Gem.

The Warg can climb the glowing stone pillars on the right side of the dungeon. Just get close to it and press the Jump button. Once at the top, kill the vampires using the Warg, and then dismount and jump through the hole in the ground.

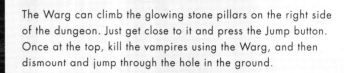

KNIGHT SCROLL, HEALTH FONT, DARK CRYSTAL

Cross the plank between the ledges at the top of the dungeon, and you can find a Knight Scroll, Health Font, and a Dark Crystal. The **Scroll** speaks of a Holy Water + Light Magic trick that creates a shield around the user.

Dungeon Battle Area 2

Follow the tunnel rooms to a small arch opening. Head through there to hang jump down to another dungeon section similar to the first area you dropped into. Here, a team of Skeleton Warriors attacks. In the back of the hallway, you can find a Stake mechanism that opens the nearby gate.

Defeat the skeletons first before attempting to open the gate. Fill up on the Neutral Elemental Fountain in the next stairwell chamber, and then climb the winding stairs up and out of the level.

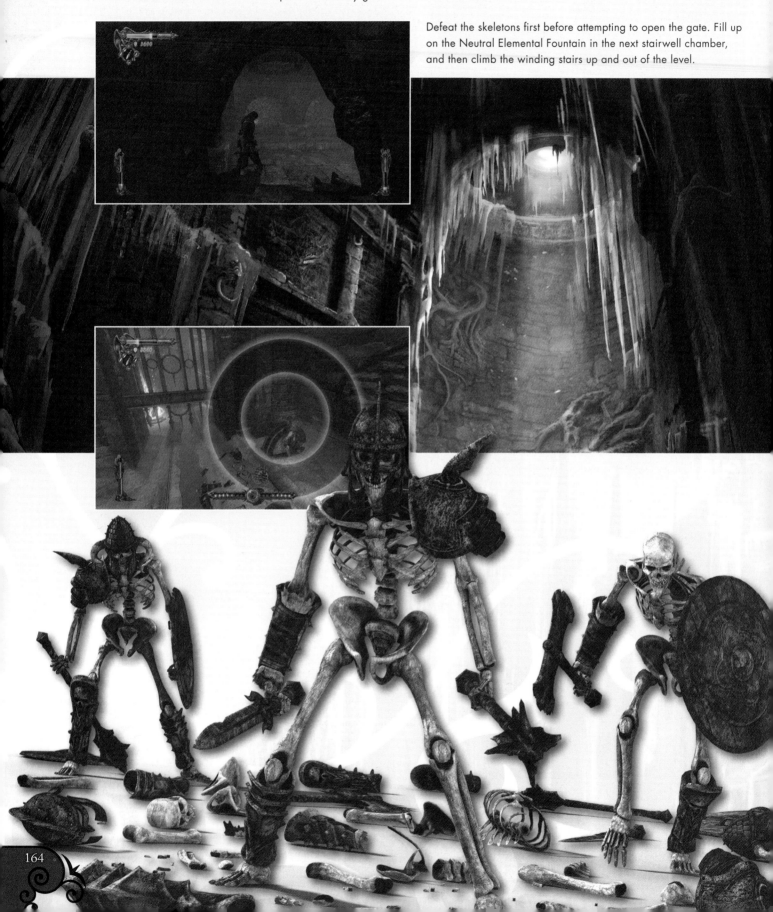

LEVEL TWO:
MAZE GARDENS

It seems getting into the castle will be more difficult than first thought. Gabriel will have to navigate the maze gardens. In this place, a man can be lost forever or devoured by the creatures that haunt its labyrinthine corridors. These gardens were once the most beautiful in all Europe, and many pilgrims would visit the castle grounds from lands far away to witness their timeless beauty. Now they lie wasted and rotten, decaying as their master lives on.

Hidden Items

‡ 1 Life Magic Gem   ‡ 1 Shadow Magic Gem

‡ 1 Light Magic Gem

Monster

‡ Mandragora   ‡ Giant Spider

Unlockable Trial

‡ Finish the level after defeating 15 Mandragoras in less than 15 seconds

Walkthrough

The Path through the Frozen Garden

Heading through the initial tunnel places you in the Maze Gardens.

Head to the right until you reach the large arch with overgrowth along its walls. Inside the arch is a tall column that you can push using the Gauntlet Punch.

Climb the column that you just moved by using its Grip ledges. You can use its Grip ledges and a simple jump to reach an adjacent column on the other side of the hedgerow.

The key that you're looking for is inside the large greenhouse building in the center of the area, but don't rush toward it yet; you need the help of one of the spiders in the area to reach the entrance.

SPIDER TIP

You can save yourself some time if, before opening the door to the greenhouse, you use the spider to break doors.

Spider Hunting

Ignore the paths that open at your left and continue toward the back right section. It is a small arena where Giant Spiders attack. Instead of killing the monster, stun and mount it.

Web Bridge

With the tamed spider, go back to the entrance, and from the edge of the gap, press the Direct Attack button to force your mount to lay a web bridge over it.

Once you have opened the path to the greenhouse, cross the web bridge to enter. Find the dead Brotherhood knight on the ground to the right as you enter. He has a puzzle-solving **Scroll**.

Beyond the knight, you find a puzzle similar to the one played during Pan's trial. Press the Use button on the glowing statue before the fountain. In this challenge, you have an unlimited number of moves to get the three statues looking at the center of the frozen fountain.

Fountain Puzzle Solution

The objective is to make all three of them look toward the center of the fountain. The basic mechanic is the same as Pan's puzzle: rotate the three puzzle sections where the movements of any one of them affect the others. There's an extra layer of difficulty: the statues spin after rotating around the fountain.

Don't get crazy thinking about movement combinations; the solution is even easier than the one from Pan's puzzle. Just move the middle statue clockwise twice. Once you've done this correctly, the key appears in the center of the fountain. The correct placement of the three statues makes the key to the castle appear in the center of the fountain. You get it automatically. Go back outside the greenhouse, crossing the web bridge again.

Exiting the Gardens

The gardens exit has a large metal door that must be broken. A spider is again the answer for this task. Find the dead knight **Scroll** just yards away from this door. It speaks of spider silk. Go to the same area where you got the spider before, attack and mount another one, and use its ranged attack on the closed door. Press the indicated button repeatedly to bend the door open with the spiderweb.

Before Dismounting or Exiting...

A couple areas from the map have hidden goodies. In the first nook, use a tamed spider to weave a web bridge over the gap. Inside the small nook, you can find a dead Brotherhood knight with a **Shadow Magic Gem**.

In the other similar nook, use the Spiked Chain to grab and pull the statue over that is blocking the secret nook. Inside is a dead knight with a **Life Magic Gem**.

Use a Shoulder Dash on the brick wall to break through and find a dead knight holding a **Light Magic Gem**.

With the path to the castle cleared, head up the stairs and use the key on the first gate. Head through the gate and you'll find yourself back in the previous area explored during the last level.

Find the daggers on the right and then sprint jump over the large gap. Use the climbing wall near the Health Font to reach the other side of the gate. Head to the front doors of the castle and use the key on the slot on the right side of the massive entrance. In a cutscene, you enter the castle.

LEVEL THREE: CASTLE HALL

Time is running out. Night is almost upon us. Soon the castle will be swarming with vampires. Those who are the most powerful of their kind are able to take on the appearance of highborn humans. Gabriel must be on his guard now, for appearances can be deceptive. I have heard that in this place, one may face ones deadliest foes without realizing it until it is too late.

Hidden Items

‡ 1 Life Magic Gem

‡ 1 Light Magic Gem

Monsters

‡ Animated Armor

‡ Vampire Warrior

Weapon Upgrade

‡ Dagger Upgrade +5

Minigame Unlock

‡ Vampire Wargame (See "Extras" from the Main Menu)

Unlockable Trial

‡ Finish the level and win the Vampire Wargame without losing more than three pieces

Walkthrough

Roasted Vampires

Once you enter the castle hall, vampires attack immediately. To stop the spawning of enemies, you have to use the power of sunlight to burn them and the holes they hide in.

As you could see outside in the previous level, the sun still shines brightly in the sky here. The only thing that prevents light from illuminating the halls are some antique tapestries hanging in front of the windows. If you move close to them, part of it glows, hinting at a possible interaction: press the Use button to use the chain on them and then pull to reveal the open window.

LIGHT FIGHT

Use the spaces created by the shafts of light to fight; most vampires avoid entering them, allowing you to attack from inside the light.

The first window's tapestry is held by nothing more than a rope. The following window is covered by three boards, which must be removed individually, one at a time. Once a board or rope is grabbed with the chain, press the button displayed repeatedly when prompted to yank it down.

The exit from this first half of the hall is locked; you can only open the gate using the Stake mechanism, but before attempting this, you need to kill all the vampires and disable the enemy generator, or there won't be enough time to complete the action.

Second Hall

In the second hall, you have to repeat the same actions that you took before, illuminating the entire area with window light. However, in this hall, you must deal with Vampire Warriors as well as a single Animated Armor. Allowing the sun to shine into the room stops the vampire generators, letting you concentrate on the puzzle that unlocks the exit door. A dead knight **Scroll** is in the back left corner. Along the right wall is another door controlled using the Stake mechanism. Open this gate and enter the next room.

Third Hall

The third hall looks almost like a chapel. Find the dead knight in the middle of the floor. He holds a **Scroll** that solves the magic rune puzzle.

Climb the rock on the left side of the room and use it to reach the alcove above. A dead Brotherhood knight holding a **Life Magic Gem** is on the ledge of this alcove.

To open the exit in this third room, you must use the two mirrors' statues (one in this third room and one in the first). So, head back to the first room if you haven't already moved the mirror to the left side of its rail and turned it to direct the light into the second hall.

Now, Gauntlet Punch the mirror statue in the third hall to the left and then punch it again along the continuing rail leading stopping in the second hall. Position the mirror so that the reflection from the first room is directed into the mirror, which is now in the second hall, and bounced into the door in the third hall. This opens the door in the third hall.

Fourth Hall

Fill up on magic energy using the Neutral Elemental Fountain in the fourth hall. Now you can solve the rune puzzle. This involves the two runes on either side of the door you just opened and the three runes inside the small nook at the back of this new room. Using the Scroll obtained by the dead knight in the previous room, you now have what you need to solve the rune puzzle.

LIGHT MAGIC GEM

Before you get to the dead knight mentioned above, look for steps that lead down, which are to the right of the cross planks. They are hard to spot from above. Continue down the stairs to find a hidden Brotherhood knight lying in a small room. He holds a **Light Magic Gem**.

Following the color code in the Scroll, hit the runes in the small nook in the fourth room with the correct magic in this order:

Rune	Description
Fourth Hall Nook	
Left Rune	Red (Shadow Magic)
Center Rune	Blue (Light Magic)
Right Rune	Blue (Light Magic)
Third Hall Door	
Left Door Column Rune	Red (Shadow Magic)
Right Door Column Rune	Red (Shadow Magic)

Puzzle Aftermath

The wall in the back of the fourth hall nook opens and clouds cover the sunlight that's kept the vampires at bay. Now as the darkness sets in, the vampires' courage and exploration increases. They soon file into your room. You must defeat a few waves of the non-stop supply of vampires before the gate in the next room opens far enough for you to escape. Throw everything you have at them, and don't spare the Holy Water. After defeating a few waves, sprint for the next large chamber and veer right for the wide staircase. Enter the next room where you'll meet a female vampire, Laura.

Vampire Wargame

Immediately after crossing the door, you'll be surprised by a young female voice. The vampire girl, Laura, is waiting for you in the games room. After the cutscene, you have the choice to play a little strategy game with her, and if you choose "yes," you won't be able to leave until you win. If you choose to skip the game, you don't win the points associated with winning the challenge.

In the center of the room, there is a giant board game, ready to be played. The objective of the game is to annihilate all the pieces of the opponent. It is a simple wargame where each player controls a vampire, a Lycanthrope, and a necromancer.

During each turn, players determine which pieces can be moved using a spinning wheel. When they lose two pieces, they are granted a second spin per turn. After losing another two, they receive a third spin.

All the pieces can either move to an empty square or attack an adjacent enemy piece during a turn. Apart from having different statistics, each piece has an extra power:

War Piece	Abilities
Vampires	Can drain life from an adjacent piece, dealing less damage but healing themselves in exchange.
Lycanthropes	Can move two squares instead of one; they also have the most powerful attacks.
Necromancers	Can summon a Zombie anywhere in the board and can attack at two squares of distance, ignoring armor value.

After the wheel stops, press Light or Shadow Magic buttons to switch between pieces of the selected type (only if more than one is available). Select a destination square for the action using the left stick, and press the appropriate button to do the desired action (the action buttons change contextually depending on the selected piece and square).

After completing the game, find the **Light Magic Gem** on the dead Brotherhood knight in the back right corner of the game board. Approach the back left corner and head through the exit to complete the level.

LEVEL FOUR:
REFECTORY

She has the body of an innocent child, yet the wits and cunning of a seasoned predator. She will kill Gabriel in a heartbeat if she could. Beautiful Laura, who was turned many centuries ago, has lived a lonely, cruel existence ever since. Gabriel will have to be very careful from now on, as he can be sure that her "mother," the one who commands here, is now fully aware of his presence and that Laura herself still has some part to play in our tale.

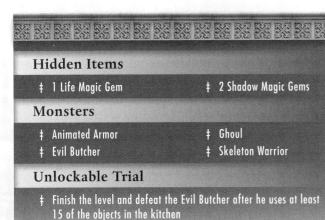

Hidden Items

‡ 1 Life Magic Gem ‡ 2 Shadow Magic Gems

Monsters

‡ Animated Armor ‡ Ghoul

‡ Evil Butcher ‡ Skeleton Warrior

Unlockable Trial

‡ Finish the level and defeat the Evil Butcher after he uses at least 15 of the objects in the kitchen

Walkthrough

Disgusting!

After the cutscene, Gabriel leaves the game room and enters the refectory. The lords who inhabited the old castle used to eat here, but now it's used by one of the few living beings that remain here, the Evil Butcher. Smash items in the initial hallway for weapons and find the Neutral Elemental Fountain just before you reach the balcony overlooking the large dining room.

While overlooking the dining room, you'll see how this monster "works." Watch as the Butcher carries some "food," to the center of the room. After that, he rings a bell, and some Ghouls appear from holes in the wall to feed on it. After that, the Butcher retires back to the kitchen.

You have to defeat the Butcher to continue. To access the kitchen, however, you must repeat the steps you saw him do in the cutscene; that is, feed the Ghouls. Defeat the Ghouls on your way down the stairs to the refectory.

Smashing the left dining table reveals a dead knight **Scroll**. The Scroll describes a much-needed key that the Butcher owns.

Feeding Ghouls

Enter the pantry through the open doorway in the back left corner of the dining room. Inside, you'll find some "food" in a glowing vat. Grab it and leave it on the glowing plate in the center of the dining hall.

With the food in its place, you can now ring the bell on the back right corner of the same room (you saw the Butcher ring it in the cinematic). During the time that the Ghoul gates remain open, use the Grip Point on the open chute door closest to the camera on the right side of the room.

Between the Walls

You enter a small passage between walls. At the first intersection, walk toward the camera to find a dead knight holding a **Shadow Magic Gem**. Then return and take the unexplored path at the previous fork to trigger a cinematic.

Boss Battle:
The Evil Butcher

You face the Evil Butcher after the introductory cutscene where he spots you and throws a butcher's knife at you (which you quickly dodge). With the combat occurring in the kitchen, this monster has the hometown advantage and uses many of the cooking items present here. The Butcher can regain health by eating a ham leg, breathe fire for some time after drinking the spicy sauce, use pieces of iron cauldrons as armor, and throw the knives scattered around the room.

BUTCHER'S DAILY SPECIALS

You have to pay attention to the Butcher whenever he decides to pick up an item, and then react accordingly to avoid suffering the effects of his special attacks.

Begin the fight throwing daggers as the Butcher approaches. His first attack could possibly be fire-blowing attack. This always occurs just after he picks up a pot of spicy sauce. Use rolling dodges to avoid this attack. Or better yet, get behind him and attack him while he's preoccupied with fire.

His normal butcher blade attacks are long-reaching, and this technique is the only thing that keeps you from using long repeated combos on him freely. So attack often with heavy combos, but just be cautious about stringing too many together so you can hit and run.

Holy Water does a number on the boss; it knocks him down and inflicts a good amount of damage. Throw all you got at him. Summon the demon from the Shadow Plane to really knock his health down.

Phase Two

When his life is almost depleted, the Butcher drinks the contents of the pot boiling on the fire and uses the pot as a helmet. This grants him immunity against your attacks. To defeat the monster, first use any aerial combo on him to make the improvised helmet spin. Then, while the Butcher remains disoriented, grab his sword (pressing Grab while it glows) and beat the minigame to finally defeat him.

While the sword is glowing, press the Grab button to use the chain on it. When prompted, press the displayed button repeatedly to struggle with it. Gabriel quickly realizes that if he lets go, the outcome would be quick and simple.

Post Boss Tasks

With the Butcher down, you can grab the Evil Butcher Key that opens the access door back to the refectory (the door to the left of the key in the kitchen). Defeat the Ghouls and enter the pantry where you found the Ghoul food.

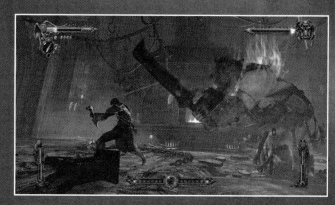

Use the key on the door in the pantry and find a **Life Magic Gem** on the dead knight inside, and take advantage of the Dark Crystal deposit on the opposite side of the room.

Head back to the start of the level, all the way back to where you entered the initial hallway. The camera facing the other way now reveals another key slot on the door you entered. Use the Butcher's key on the door, and move forward to enter a new fight against Skeleton Warriors and an Animated Armor.

To leave this arena, you have to solve a new magic runes puzzle. The hint Scroll for this puzzle can be found on the top floor of this puzzle chamber. To reach it, climb using a Grip Point visible in one of the walls when standing on the ruined steps on the right side of the room.

Climb the scaffold to reach the top level with the large hole in the floor. Find a Neutral Elemental Fountain near the large statue. Find the puzzle-solving **Scroll** in the altar below the large statue. Cross the broken wooden floor frame pieces to reach the opposite side of the room. Enter a connecting room to find the dead knight with a **Shadow Magic Gem**.

Return to the lower floor by retracing the same route you took to get up on the top floor. Once down, you can solve the rune puzzle using the hint Scroll you just found. The three runes on the left side of the room (under the statues) should be from left to right: Blue, Blue, Red. The runes on the right side of the room should be: Red, Blue, Red to complete the puzzle. Head through the now-opened exit between the runes.

CHAPTER VII

LEVEL ONE: BALCONY

The Butcher who commanded the castle kitchens feeds the corpses of the dead to the Ghouls. The efficiency of the Queen's household is formidable indeed. The vampires drain the blood and the Ghouls feed on the remains, nothing is left. Using his powers is making Gabriel far stronger than I anticipated. He will need more than physical prowess when he faces her. She can put a glamour upon his hear that will tempt him to forget everything he knows, even his beloved. She holds the next piece of the mask, and I fear that he will fall at the last.

Hidden Items

‡ 1 Light Magic Gem   ‡ 2 Shadow Magic Gem

Monsters

‡ Skeleton Warrior   ‡ Vampire Warrior
‡ Swordmaster

Unlockable Trial

‡ Finish the level after beating the logic gates puzzle in seven movements

Walkthrough

Outside in the Cold

After leaving the refectory, Gabriel is back outside the castle. Take your time to deal with a few Vampire Warriors, and head to the left side of the balcony. The camera changes position, showing the broken edge of the platform; use it to descend to the level below. You land on some wooden beams arranged forming a path through the gap, which can be crossed.

Halfway through the wooden boards path, you'll see a dead Brotherhood knight on your right. You can't jump to him from the beams; just continue forward, and you'll reach it.

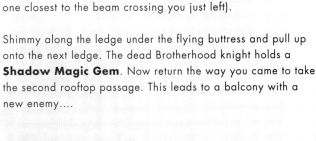

As soon as you step off the last beam, there are two exits to your right separated by a dividing wall that is easily overcome by walking along the snow-covered, slanted rooftop. To get to the dead knight you saw, drop down through the first exit (the one closest to the beam crossing you just left).

Shimmy along the ledge under the flying buttress and pull up onto the next ledge. The dead Brotherhood knight holds a **Shadow Magic Gem**. Now return the way you came to take the second rooftop passage. This leads to a balcony with a new enemy....

Swordmaster Balcony

After crossing the gap in the roof, you enter a balcony where three Swordmasters attack you. Deal with them (the vials of Holy Water work especially well against these enemies), and get close to the rear wall. Looking at it, you soon realize that there are columns to the left that you can grab onto; use them to climb up to the next rooftop.

Rooftop

Continue forward along the rooftop path until you come to a locked gate. The key is on the lower floor. Look to the right of this locked gate to find the **Scroll** on the dead knight.

To get the key for this gate, go back around the building until you reach an area where the handrail is broken. This is positioned to the left of the broken rail area you came up from the balcony through.

Hang off the edge of the rooftop and shimmy right until you see a Grip Point above your head. Use this to lower yourself to first see an open window and also to see another Grip ledge on the next column on the other side of the window. If you want health and a Scroll, then enter the window below (there's also a Swordmaster inside). If you wish to just continue to get the key, then grapple to the next Grip ledge.

First Window: Health Font, Scroll, Swordmaster

The room through this window holds the key, but you'll discover that the room is divided in two by a metal gate, and the key is on the other side. Entering the room allows you to reach a dead knight with a **Scroll**, but it also initiates a fight with a Swordmaster. You can also find a Health Font if you head all the way toward the camera in this short room.

Second Window: Key

Grapple halfway to the top of the chain and then jump against the wall and back to reach a ledge on the other side. Then, border the column and go down to enter the second room. You find the key inside.

Quickly take the **Light Magic Gem** from the dead knight on the middle of the floor. Two Skeleton Warriors animate and attack. Take them out to earn the key they hold. Once you have acquired the key, retrace your steps back to the rooftop at the locked gate; open the door and advance up the brick wall straight ahead and enter the next chamber.

A Vintage Artifact

Gabriel stands in a room with old furniture and stuff covered with dusty drapes. There is a metal door in one of the walls, which can be opened by solving a toy puzzle. Before you begin the puzzle game, find the dead knight to the left of the puzzle wall near the tall draped object. This **Scroll** gives you the solution to the puzzle (at a price of not receiving points once solving it). Also, you can find another knight that holds a **Shadow Magic Gem** behind the row of junk on the right of the room.

Solving the Logic Gate Puzzle

To interact with the puzzle, get close to the object until it glows and press the Grab button. You then find a system of levers and walls. Moving the left stick left or right highlights one of the three balls at the top of the board. The Jump button drops the selected ball. The ball bounces down through the maze and switches the position of any levers it touches. The levers glow when they are in the correct position; your objective is to switch all the levers in the maze.

There is no time or move limit to solve this puzzle, and randomly dropping balls throughout the board usually won't be enough to do it, so relax and preview the path the ball will take before releasing it.

HINT SCROLL SOLUTION

There are three slots to drop the ball down. Drop the ball down in the selected slots in this order to solve the puzzle: 1, 2, 2, 2, 2, 2, 3. Once the puzzle is solved, the camera shows the gate while it opens, and you are now free to continue through the new passage to the end of the level.

LEVEL TWO: ELECTRIC LABORATORY

This part of the castle was once where acclaimed scientist Friedrich von Frankenstein conducted his experiments into artificial life. He was quite mad and often would conduct horrific and depraved acts trying to discover the secrets of life itself. His own demise was equally gruesome. The Vampire Queen took him, but kept him alive. Thus over many centuries, she fed on him daily, keeping him at the brink of death, yet living and aware. Why she did this is only known to a few…she once loved life and loved living things and, before she became a lord of shadow, she vowed she would punish Frankenstein for his vile acts. As a Dark Lord, she was able to keep her word.

Hidden Items

‡ 1 Life Magic Gem   ‡ 1 Light Magic Gem

Monsters

‡ Mechanical Monstrosity

Unlockable Trial

‡ Finish the level and deactivate the Mechanical Monstrosity using only the Tesla coil in the lab after it is activated

Walkthrough

Short Circuit

You find yourself in the infamous Friedrich von Frankenstein's laboratory, surrounded by strange machines connected by bolts of electricity. These electric fields are dangerous, so you should try to avoid moving too close to them. The glowing devices connect only with neighbors of the opposite charge. Pick up the **Scroll** from the dead Brotherhood knight lying below the nearest electrical hazard. His scroll describes the next puzzle, and if you desire, solves it as well.

The knight writes: "...the strange devices create deadly barriers between the red and blue ones; now I only need to find a way to make them switch colors..."

In this area, some switches in the ground allow you to manipulate the electric charges by pressing them with the Earthquake Punch (hold the Block button and press and hold the Area Attack button to perform the move). You can also press those that are placed in walls with Shadow Magic charged daggers.

Electric Labyrinth Solved

ELECTRIC ROOM 1

So, to make it to the next hallway through the electric charges, Earthquake Punch the first switch **(1)** on the left to make it safe to reach the next floor switch on the right. Punch the middle **(2)** one and then the last one **(3)** on the left to reach the hallway safely.

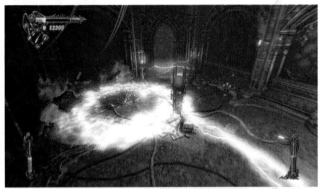

SWITCH CABLES

You can predict the results of using a switch by looking at the cables that connect them to the electric terminals. Remember that only devices with an opposite charge create an electricity bolt.

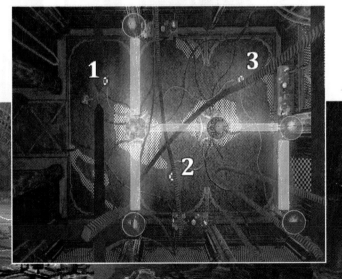

ELECTRIC ROOM 2

Once out of the first room and through the hallway, you'll reach a much bigger room with a more intricate electricity puzzle.

Start by punching the switch **(1)** where you enter. It makes the lamp sitting on the rail move right, closing one path while opening the other. Find the dead knight in the left corner with the **Shadow Magic Gem**. Now head to **(2)**, and punch the deactivated lamp device all the way along its own rail. You have to punch **(1)** again to move the previous lamp back along its rail heading left this time.

Continue punching the device on the rail around the corner to its final destination at the end of the rail at position **(3)**. Once the lamp gets to its destination, it opens the path to **(4)**. Punch the wall switch there, and it opens the way to the exit. Punch floor switch **(1)** again to reach area **(5)**.

Fill up on magic using the Neutral Elemental Fountain, and take some daggers from the glowing bag after getting to **(5)**. Here you discover that using switch **(4)** not only opens the exit but also closes the path to it.

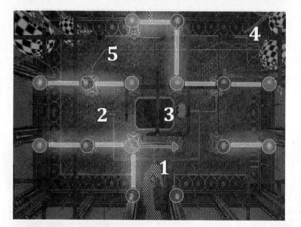

Fortunately, from this position **(5)**, you can use the throwing daggers imbued with Shadow Magic to activate the switch. Throw them once to move toward the exit and then a second time to make the exit accessible. Now, head on to the third and last part of the electric labyrinth.

ELECTRIC ROOM 3

Advance toward the device at **(1)**, but don't use it yet. Instead, turn left towards the destructible wall at **(2)**, and smash it down with the shoulder charge. You find another floor switch behind it. Punch it and get the **Red Lens** for the chromatic observatory at **(3)** by punching the floor switch next to it. Taking the Red Lens also releases the Mechanical Monstrosity...

Boss Battle:
The Mechanical Monstrosity

Once the fight starts, you cannot leave the combat arena; to defeat this monster, you have to take advantage of the way the labyrinth operates. After damaging the monster, it tries to recharge its batteries by connecting its rear end to one of the electric devices hanging from the ceiling in the center of the combat arena.

Run to the floor switch shown in the cinematic and then Earthquake Punch the switch to overcharge the lamp while the monster is using it. Instead of recharging its health, the lamp damages the boss. After repeating this process a few times, the monster falls, defeated.

With the monster destroyed and the Red Lens in your hands, you now have what it takes to get to the observatory.

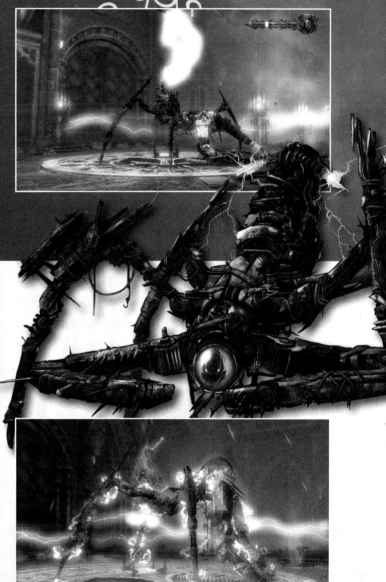

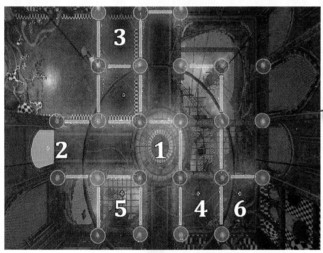

ELECTRIC ROOM 3 CONTINUED

Acquiring the Red Lens activates the Mechanical Monstrosity. After defeating it, go back to the rotating mechanism **(1)** and rotate it 180 degrees until the blue lamp is in the lower left position. This opens the path to **(4)**. Punch floor switch **(4)** and then go back to the central device and turn it until you can go to **(5)**; this floor switch enables access to **(6)**.

Use the moving floor plate in the back right corner to reach the dead knight in the corner holding the **Life Magic Gem**.

Continue riding the floor plate to the end of its rail and access switch **(6)**. Punching this floor switch opens the exit gate near **(3)**. As you leave, the boss is seen getting back on its feet.

PUZZLE SOLVED!

LEVEL THREE:
CHROMATIC OBSERVATORY

Gabriel has finally defeated Frankenstein's abomination. This hellish place is enough to thwart any man's resolve, and yet Gabriel seems completely willing to continue to the bitter end. I hardly recognize my old friend now. A steely resolve has taken hold, and compassion is now gone from his heart. He doesn't sleep these days, more's the pity. He just rages at the world and those creatures that dare to confront him. This next challenge will tax his mind further, and I fear it may break it forever.

Hidden Items

‡ 1 Life Magic Gem   ‡ 1 Shadow Magic Gem
‡ 1 Light Magic Gem

Monster

‡ Animated Armor   ‡ Swordmaster
‡ Deadly Toys   ‡ Vampire Warrior

Unlockable Trial

‡ Finish the level, destroying two Deadly Toys using normal hits before completely killing any of them with a Grip

Walkthrough

Moonlight Lens Machine

Begin this level by partaking in the Health Font and the Neutral Elemental Fountain found at the entrance of this large hall. If you get here without the red lens, which can be acquired in the last level of the electric labyrinth, you won't be able to manipulate the pieces of this puzzle.

This room has five doors, distributed equally along the exterior circumference; in the center, a large machine similar to a telescope stands silently, pointing at the sky. Each one of the doors' connecting rooms (except the one used to enter the area) has a colored gem over it. The color matches the carpet in front of each door, as well.

Using the machine in the center of the room as well as some magic lenses scattered around the level opens the doors in this room: the telescope gathers the moonlight entering through the dome and tints it when it crosses the different lenses. The colored ray can hit the gems over the doors, and if the gem has the correct color, then the ray can open the door.

LENS MACHINE OPERATION

Push the left stick up and down to select one of the lenses of the telescope. Press the Use button to insert or remove the selected disc from the trajectory of the moonlight ray. The combination of inserted lenses determines the color of the ray and subsequently the door opened by it. The solution of the observatory puzzle:

ANIMATED ARMOR ACTIVATION: LIGHT MAGIC GEM

Two of the combinations (**CYAN** and **BLUE**) don't open any of the doors. Instead, they activate Animated Armors in the telescope room. Find the **Light Magic Gem** on the dead knight lying on the floor against the wall on the right side of the purple carpet. Triggering the Animated Armors allows you to get to this knight hidden behind one of the Armors.

‡ You can get the **RED LENS** in the last room of the electric labyrinth.
‡ Use the **RED LENS** in the telescope to open the **RED DOOR**.
‡ Inside the Red Chamber, you can find the **GREEN LENS**.
‡ Combining the **RED** and **GREEN LENS** allows you to open the **YELLOW DOOR**.
‡ Inside the Yellow Chamber, you can find the **BLUE LENS**.
‡ Combining the **RED** and **BLUE LENSES** allows you to open the **VIOLET DOOR**, where the Vampire Child is waiting for you.

Your objective is to access the Violet Chamber, home of the Vampire Child. However, to open her door, you have to enter at least two of the other colored rooms:

Red Chamber

Find a dead knight in the middle of the floor. He holds a hint **Scroll** that solves the puzzle in the room. He attempted lighting a Shadow Gem in one of the corners but said he was too slow to do the rest. Defeat the Vampire Warriors in the room, and then attempt the room puzzle.

The **Green Lens** is inside this Red Chamber, behind a closed door in the back of the room. Four symbols are painted on the ground in corners around the dead knight; these suggest some kind of magic trickery. To open the door, you have to light the four corner symbols all at once using the power of Dark Magic. However, the symbols won't stay charged for long, so the only way to achieve this is by using the Shoulder Charge.

While Shadow Magic is enabled, Shoulder Charge from corner to corner until the entire square is lit. Once all four corners are glowing with Shadow Magic at the same time, the door opens.

Once you complete the floor puzzle, the back room opens. Take the lens from the dead knight on the floor. The gate is closed, locking you in the small room with a Swordmaster. Defeat the single Swordmaster to reopen the gate. Return to the telescope mechanism in the first room.

Yellow Chamber

Defeat the Vampire Warriors in the Yellow Chamber. Here, you find the **Blue Lens**, protected by another puzzle, identical in mechanic to the previous one. This time, the shape that you must "draw" with the dash movement is slightly harder to solve.

Again, after getting the Lens, the door closes. On this occasion, two Swordmasters spawn to attack.

Green Chamber: Magic Gem and White Lens

Enter the Green Room and then grapple over a large hole in the floor using the Hook Tip. Next, jump at the end of your swing jump using the Seraph Shoulders to make it to the other side without falling in the extra long pit.

To the left (camera faces you) of the new side of the pit is a dead knight with the **Life Magic Gem**. Here, you also see a new Shoulder Dash puzzle. Complete the zigzag pattern with Shadow Magic enabled to finish the puzzle. This unlocks the White Key, which floats above an emblem on the floor within the current floor puzzle. Pick up the key and head to the White Room.

White Chamber

Set the machine to unlock the White Chamber and head inside. Find the dead knight on the right end of the initial balcony inside. His **Scroll** tells an interesting story.

On the opposite end of the balcony, you can find a high Grip Point. Use the Hook Tip to grapple from this to the ledge above. Follow the scaffold to another high Grip Point. Use this to reach the highest scaffold. Follow the narrow boards across the room. Use the last Grip Point to lower you back down to the floor level. Use the White Key in the nearby lock. Enter the unlocked room to take the **Shadow Magic Gem** from the dead knight in the middle of the floor. Backtrack along the same course to get you back to the lens machine room.

Deadly Toys

Gabriel doesn't fight directly against the Vampire Child. As you enter the Violet Room, in a short cutscene, the vampire summons some of her large toys and then vanishes afterwards. These new enemies are ragdolls, diabolic monsters animated with the dark power of the vampire.

To *completely* destroy the Deadly Toys, normal hits won't be enough; you have to finish them with a Grip move when they begin to glow, and also beat the minigame associated with the Grip. Successfully completing the halo ring challenge results in Gabriel ripping the life source out of the toys' chest stuffing. Otherwise, the magic energy that empowers them flees upward, where it animates a new Deadly Toy.

DARK OIL

Watch out for the dark oil that the ragdolls vomit from time to time. This ooze can trap Gabriel, leaving him defenseless against the ragdolls' attacks. To break free from the oil, press the indicated button repeatedly.

Once all the Deadly Toys are annihilated, a cutscene plays. The Vampire Child directly attacks Gabriel, and only the love of Marie stops her from completing the job.

CHAPTER VIII

LEVEL ONE: OUTER WALL

Curious, isn't it? Love can be a powerful weapon it seems, even to those who are dead. Laura has spared him. Though she has the power to take his life, she has given it back, and all for love. Perhaps she remembers her true mother's arms around her, comforting her before she became this creature. Perhaps she remembers the feelings of love thought long lost to her heart all those years ago. A child's love is without bitterness or boundaries, a pure love. I wonder what will become of her, this lost soul, when we kill her present "mother" and send her to the pits of hell where she belongs?

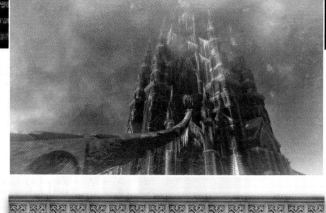

Hidden Items

‡ 1 Light Magic Gem ‡ 1 Shadow Magic Gem

Monsters

‡ Gremlin ‡ Swordmaster

‡ Skeleton Warrior ‡ Vampire Warrior

Unlockable Trial

‡ Finish the level after killing 10 Gremlins using only your silver daggers

Walkthrough

Waylay at the Tower Top

Gabriel is getting closer to the second Dark Lord. You start the level on the balcony of the Vampire Child's chamber from the previous level. Find a **Scroll** on the dead Brotherhood knight on the same ledge with you. Hang off the right side of the balcony by accessing the Grip ledge through the broken balcony rail.

Shimmy to the end, hand jump across a gap, and continue around a corner so you can jump backward to a Grip ledge behind you. Once on the large column, you'll find a high Grip Point that you can use to grapple climb to a higher ledge. Another Grip Point appears up the same column. Repeat this pattern until you have reached the rooftop balcony, where you can find a Health Font.

Jump up onto the next higher balcony and immediately explore the left corner of this new platform. In a nook, the camera pans closely to a glowing dead Brotherhood knight. This soldier holds a **Shadow Magic Gem**.

On the opposite end of the balcony, you see a dead knight with a hint **Scroll** that solves the gate exit rune puzzle. Also, you can find a Neutral Elemental Fountain nearby.

Once you approach the locked gate to the right of the dead soldier that held the hint Scroll, Vampire Warriors and Skeleton Warriors attack. These enemies spawn and attack continually, so you must solve the gate rune puzzle between attack waves. If you run out of magic energy to work the puzzle, recharge using the enemies' energy.

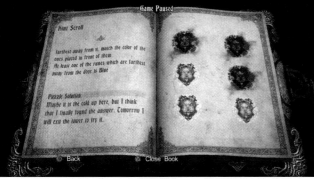

Solving the Rune Puzzle

So you don't have to waste points solving the rune puzzle by using the knight's Scroll, take a look here... these are the knight's graphic tips:

There are three runes on the left of the gate and three on the right. From left to right on the left side you must turn the runes with these colors in order: Blue, Blue, Red. While on the right side of the gate from left to right (starting with the closest one to the gate): Red, Red, Blue.

Chained Path to the Tower

Once the puzzle is solved, refill your magic using the nearby fountain and then exit through the now opened gate. Continue toward the Vampire Queen's sanctorum. The only path available is through the large metal chain that connects both towers.

Halfway to the castle, things get complicated: there is a large platform in the center of the support chain preventing you from reaching the continuing chain to the castle. A metal fence with a single opening, which allows you to enter the platform but not exit the way you need to go, surrounds this platform.

As soon as you cross the doorway in the gate, some Gremlins start attacking in groups, giving you some time between waves to find an exit to the platform. It's best to just defeat all the Gremlins and work on the puzzle in peace.

In the center of the platform, there is a rotating mechanism that you can turn. To exit the platform and reach the other side of the continuing chain pathway, you have to turn the mechanism to rotate the fence around its perimeter. This moves the doorway in the gate to the opposite edge of the platform. However, as soon as you release the handle, the door quickly rolls back to its original position (along with the rest of the gate, of course). You have to hurry up and run toward the door so you can jump at the midway point to find a side path and some stairs that lead to a secret room.

SPRINT OR DASH

To reach the door before it returns back, you need to use the boots' Sprint (double tap the left stick in the desired direction), but it is easier if you activate the Dark Magic and use the Shoulder Dash (press and hold Block button, then push the left stick in the direction of the door).

Secret Tower Key Room

After leaving the platform, the chain pathway directly connects to the main tower. However, the access gate is locked, and you need a Tower Key to open it. When you make it through the doorway on the chain platform, follow the low path through a tunnel that leads underneath the platform.

The **Tower Key**, protected by a pair of Swordmasters, is on a fallen Brotherhood knight found on the floor close to the camera near the front windows. After getting rid of the two enemies, use the rotating device inside the room to reopen the exit out of this chamber.

Follow the continuing chain pathway to the castle. In the locked gate chamber, you can find a Health Font on the side near the key slot and a dead knight on the opposite side of the room. He holds a **Light Magic Gem**. Now, use the Tower Key on the keyhole and head through the doorway at the top of the stairs to complete the level.

LEVEL TWO: THE CLOCKWORK TOWER

The vampire's mercy is playing on his thoughts, I see that clearly on his face. Perhaps Laura reminded him of poor Claudia? Seeing his beloved Marie again has brought it all back to him. Marie's love is all he has now, and the hope of holding her again, the only hope. He is close now, close to the bitch who commands these vampire vermin. Gabriel will make her pay for the injustices he has felt at her hands. She is powerful, she will try every trick in the book to tempt him to her cause. There is just the small matter of the clockwork tower to overcome first. Another mad invention of Frankenstein that I hope will only delay his sweet revenge.

Hidden Items

‡ 1 Life Magic Gem   ‡ 1 Light Magic Gem

Monsters

‡ Mechanical Monstrosity

Unlockable Trial

‡ Finish the level and get to the top corridor in less than five minutes

Walkthrough

Vampire Tower: First Floor

The interior of the Vampire Queen's tower is like a giant clock full of gears plus moving platforms; all the movements here have to be measured carefully, as a fall to the bottomless pit below is fatal.

A large, round, hanging platform occupies the center of the tower. This platform has three branches parting from it, which serve to connect to the tower boundary. You can reach the central platform using the wooden planks, walking while keeping your balance by using the "Hold" button when prompted.

From the center platform, continue forward, ignoring the left path. Once you've reached the small ledge at the opposite side of the tower, you see a moving platform at your right. This platform transports you to a giant gear, which rotates counterclockwise. Jump on the closest tooth and get ready to jump again before it reaches the wall, vaulting over to a Grip ledge on the wall.

HIDDEN LIGHT MAGIC GEM

Once you have Seraph Shoulders, jump from the first platform reached at the end of the plank leading away from the center lift platform. Jump off the left edge of the fixed ledge and use the Seraph Shoulders to reach a previously unseen similar ledge. Here, you find a dead knight with the Light Magic Gem.

Hand jump through the moving gear on the wall and continue through a similar puzzle until you reach a lift platform that takes you to a ledge with a rotating device on it.

Vampire Tower: Second Floor

Gabriel stands on a high platform with a rotating mechanism. Here, you can safely turn the device until the central platform has risen completely and a save icon appears. New planks reach out to meet your ledge from the raised platform.

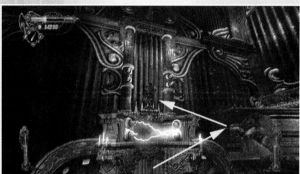

With the central platform placed at the same height, you can again walk along the plank towards the center platform. Once you reach the center platform, turn left and walk the plank to the ledge on the left.

There is a very difficult electric wall to grapple up behind this ledge. Attach the Hook Tip to the high Grip Point, and then walk up the rope as close as you can get to the lowest electricity bolt on the wall. Time your jump so that you'll land just above the closest bolt when the second bolt above is turning off. To do this you have to wall kick off the wall as hard as you can and then move up the rope as you swing out.

Once you reach the Grip Point, use the adjacent ledges to the right to shimmy to the corner. The only way to continue is by jumping to a moving platform below. Almost immediately after landing, prepare to jump to a small, fixed platform.

While on the fixed platform, look at the movement of the platform you just left and try to jump on it again on the opposite side of the fixed ledge.

Before it enters the wall, do a third jump toward the Grip ledge above the electric wheel. Shimmy right to the next fixed ledge.

Jump from the second box seat-like balcony to the Grip ledge above the electric rotating gear. Shimmy along the ledge as far as you can around a corner and then do a backwards jump to the next ledge. Pull up and jump to a fixed ledge with an electric wall and a Neutral Elemental Fountain.

The Neutral Elemental Fountain ledge has an electric wall climbing challenge similar to the earlier one. This time, there's no grapple, so simply time your movement up the Grip ledges with the turning off of the electric bolts.

The Neutral Elemental Fountain ledge has an electric wall climbing challenge similar to the earlier one. This time, there's no grapple, so simply time your movement up the Grip ledges with the turning off of the electric bolts.

Jump to the highest Grip ledge and shimmy over the ledge on the left and drop. Leap over the electric wall gap to the right ledge to get the **Life Magic Gem** from the dead Brotherhood knight there.

Grapple to the last large ledge to the left. Find the rotating device on the edge of the ledge and start turning it to raise the center platform to your new floor. While you're doing this, the Mechanical Monstrosity attacks. Let go and fight....

Revenge of the Machines

While fighting the Mechanical Monstrosity, keep in mind that you haven't seen all its tricks until now. The mechanical beast has an extra attack this time; it makes the debris scattered around the room float around it, using the machinery pieces as ammunition to throw at you from time to time. However, this time, the fight doesn't take place in the laboratory, so the monster has no place to recharge its batteries.

If you have the Dark Crystals for it, summon the demon from the Shadow Plane to attack; this move takes a quarter of the boss's health. When the boss reaches a quarter health remaining, it becomes invincible with normal attacks and displays a gray health bar. This means that a grab attack is in order.

The Grab attack begins with a halo ring challenge to successfully stomp its head to the ground while riding on its back. This is followed by the exact same move, a second head stomp!

Next, you roll off the front of the beast and have to complete the halo challenge to successfully punch it in the head. This shatters the cockpit and releases some green gas that stabilizes the life form inside controlling the machine. You rip the hairless life form from the machine and smash its little head with one hand until it explodes.

After beating the enemy, use the rotating device to raise the platform up to your floor and then cross the plank to reach the center platform. The platform begins to lift, and the mission ends successfully.

LEVEL THREE: OLROX

The giant mechanisms and gears continue to turn, but Gabriel continues to foil them. He is now in the heart of evil. Darkness is all around, surrounding him from all sides. Here, he will meet the brother of the one he destroyed in the village. His name is Olrox. The two brothers have been her greatest champions, yet I sense their reign of evil is ending here tonight. Olrox and his brother Brauner are traitors who took sides with the Queen when she became one of the Dark Lords. He has wreaked terror on the lands ever since, but now he will meet one who is greater, more powerful than he. One who will deliver a message without any mercy. Olrox, meet Gabriel Belmont and his Vampire Killer.

Hidden Items

‡ 1 Shadow Magic Gem

Monsters

‡ Commander Olrox

Unlockable Trial

‡ Finish the level after keeping the focus meter at its maximum value for 60 seconds

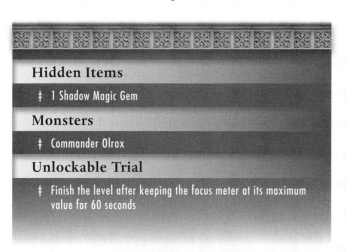

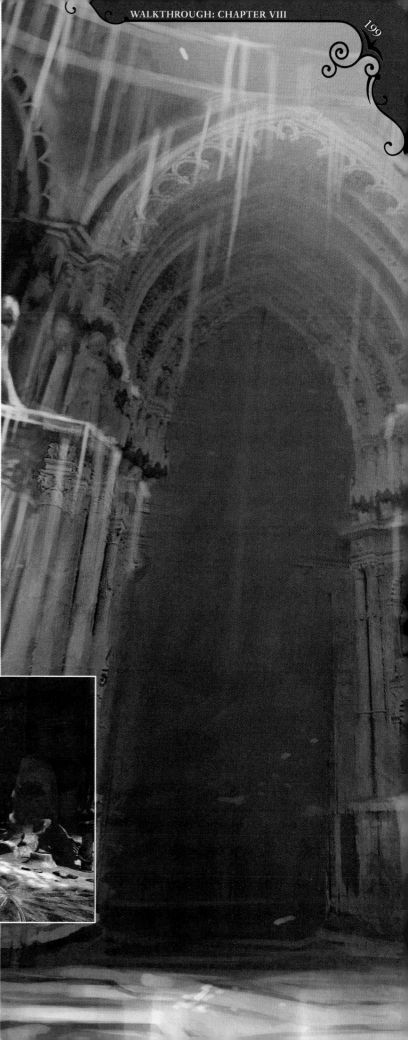

Boss Battle: Commander Olrox

Gabriel finally gets to the top of the tower of the Vampire Queen; only two obstacles remain between you and the second Dark Lord... The first one is the second of the Vampire's lieutenants, Commander Olrox, who is waiting for you at the top corridor. As soon as the platform arrives, he fiercely greets you.

The second Elite Vampire is better prepared than his predecessor. He's equipped with a flame blade and likes to grab you and suck blood from your neck. When the boss performs a grab move, press the indicated button repeatedly to break free and issue a counterattack that does a little damage to the boss.

The dual flame blades are thrown just after a warning is given. The warnings: "My Lady will be pleased after I bring her your head!" Or, "How dare you challenge my Lady?" When you hear this, you should Dash or just start running very fast from the way the boss is facing to avoid the thrown blades.

Luckily, with his victims, the boss only accumulates a quarter health. To take out the victims, you must attack the boss as he sucks their blood to force him away. Quickly attack the victim in the iron maiden until it splatters. The first is a Lycan, and the second is a Brotherhood knight. The only way to get into the iron maidens is to beat the boss down to close to nothing and wait for him to pry them open them for a blood refill. So follow him each time until you have destroyed both of the Lycans.

The next time you knock the boss's health down to a gray bar, the Grab finishing move challenge begins. Successfully execute the halo ring challenge each time it appears, and you will block two blade attacks, struggle for domination on the second weapon-locking strike, club the boss in the side of the head with the hilt of your cross, steel his blade, and finally like his predecessor, you kill him with his own weapon. His own blood drains into the puzzle circle in the middle of the arena.

Blood Puzzle

After Commander Olrox is vanquished, his blood unlocks a puzzle hidden in the elevator platform that you used to get here. The objective of this puzzle is to use the blood to trace a route on the maze. Before you continue further, head to the second victim's iron maiden and take the **Shadow Magic Gem** from the dead Brotherhood knight. A hint **Scroll** is actually retrieved from the glowing puzzle itself. This has the solution for the puzzle for you if you wish to take the chance of losing the credits for solving it yourself.

The task that the puzzle proposes seems very easy, but here is the catch: the time allotted to get from one point to the next is limited, so not every possible path is valid, with some of them being longer than others.

You are using the circular spots in the maze as checkpoints: whenever you get to any of them, all the blood from the path fills it, resetting the amount of time available to get to the next checkpoint. Here is the complete path with all the checkpoints numbered in the visit order that creates the shortest route possible to the top:

Once the puzzle is solved, the door to the vampire chambers opens, leaving you one step closer to reclaiming the power of the second Dark Lord. Head through the door to end the level.

LEVEL FOUR:
THE THRONE ROOM

The blood of Olrox has opened the way to the Queen. She holds the next piece of the God mask, which Gabriel must acquire, if he is to be with his beloved again. She will try to seduce him, to glamour him, but he will see through her mask, I am sure of it. He is so very strong now and even she must fear her own death at his hands. I can smell her fear, her stench. Vampires can sense the living, but the dead she cannot. She knows Gabriel is here, yet she cannot sense death close at hand also. She knows what it is he wants. Poor, beautiful Carmilla, you will cry bloody tears before this night has ended!

Hidden Items

‡ 1 Light Magic Gem

Relics

‡ Seraph Shoulders

Monsters

‡ Vampire Dark Lord   ‡ Vampire Warrior

Unlockable Trial

‡ Finish the level and defeat the Dark Lord after she kills at least two of her own Vampire Warriors

Boss Battle:
Vampire Dark Lord

"The Queen of Vampires"

You begin this mission facing the long stairs up to the Queen's castle. Make sure to take advantage of the Health Font and the Neutral Elemental Fountain at the foot of the stairs. A dead Brotherhood knight holding a **Light Magic Gem** can be found halfway up and on the right side of the stairs, at the edge of a reoccurring lightning shadow.

The Queen's throne room is at the top of the stairs. The Vampire Queen awaits your arrival. Upon your entrance, she is introduced in a cutscene. After trying to seduce you and failing miserably, the combat begins.

Stage One

In the first stage of battle, the Vampire Dark Lord remains in her human form, shooting energy rays at you from time to time. You cannot damage her during this stage; instead, you have to kill all the Vampire Warriors that appear in the combat arena. Strategically, switch from Shadow to Light Magic to increase damage and then to heal.

Stage Two

Once all the warriors are defeated, the Queen transforms into a giant vampire monster. The second phase starts with the Queen using her powers to destroy a large part of the floor, leaving behind huge cracks that you can jump on to move across the area. From now on, she directly attacks you, using both melee attacks and her magic powers.

The two of you aren't alone in this fight, either. Along with fighting the ugly form of the Queen, you also need to continue fending off her Vampire Warrior minions. Run from the boss. Avoid her. Concentrate all your attacks on the minions to get them out of the way so you can direct your full attention to the boss once they are dead.

Use your favorite most damaging moves on the Queen while being faithful to your dodge maneuvers to keep your own damage down to a minimum. When she is around half empty of life, she starts glowing. Press the Use button to begin the halo ring combo challenge.

Before you begin the challenge, you should know that if you fail to execute any of the moves in the halo ring combo, the Queen bites you and sucks your blood. This allows her to regain some health.

The first move is three stabs to the neck, when executed properly. The second move is two thrusts to the abdomen with the Combat Cross. The next move is an uppercut to the bottom of her jaw, which comes back down onto the back of her neck. Now crumpled over, you remove the cross, and she escapes. A checkpoint is reached, and the last stage begins.

Stage Three

Stage three is much like the previous stage, only the boss adds in an attack where she flies up in the air and releases a team of bats that perform a flyby attack on you. This can be easily dodged.

She also flies up in the air and releases a large area of effect electric shockwave. This can be avoided by getting into the air while this covers the ground. So, whenever the boss flies into the air, be prepared to let offense take a backseat to defense.

Stage Four

Once the vampire is badly injured a fourth time, she'll surround herself in a magic protection sphere that grants her immunity against damage and casts a powerful energy blast towards you. This attack triggers a resistance minigame that, if beaten, ends with you absorbing the energy from the attack using the gauntlet. Simply press the button indicated repeatedly to win this challenge.

The attack left the Queen stunned for a short time, but still encased inside her magic shield. The only way to destroy it involves using any of the gauntlet attacks, while it's still charged with the vampire's energy. Any one of these begins the final minigame sequence.

While she is down, you take the opportunity to stab the Queen in the back. She kicks you off her as she flies away. You sprint and catch onto her as she flies skyward. She manages to kick you off after gaining a good amount of altitude. The first halo ring challenge comes just after you begin to fall.

Successfully beating the first ring challenge allows you to launch and impale the Queen with your Spiked Chain.

After being taken on a flight around the castle while attached by a chain to the wounded Queen Vampire, you take the opportunity to plant your feet on the tallest rooftop as it comes into range. You use the leverage to stop and pull the Queen as she tries to escape. Beat the halo challenge to continue holding onto the big catch.

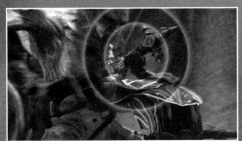

Performing this move successfully results in the Queen being impaled on the sharp end of the rooftop needle. With one last big, herculean pull, the vampire is pulled down as far as possible on the rooftop needle, and the entire castle crumbles under pressure.

Since that wasn't enough to kill her, once everyone ends up on the ground again, the boss stumbles to her feet with a nasty abdominal and chest wound.

The next halo challenge is to put your Spike through her heart. Done correctly, the battle continues as you struggle to rip the Stake out of her heart.

Complete the halo challenge during this scene, and you rip the Stake out, allowing a fountain of blood to spew from her evaporating body. With that done...you've earned your wings. "Seraph Shoulders" to be exact.

CHAPTER IX

LEVEL ONE:
BONES FOREST

So Pan comes again with words of wisdom and advice for our hero. Gabriel is angry now, Carmilla's betrayal has made him question his own faith. The brotherhood means nothing to him anymore. He only wants his Marie back. He now has two pieces of the mask and only one more to find to make it complete. He must travel now to the Land of the Dead, and he must face the final Lord, Death himself. There are still many leagues to travel, and I cannot risk being seen, for I doubt even one of his brotherhood could help him now. He must go where none may follow...into the abyss.

Hidden Items

‡ 1 Life Magic Gem	‡ 2 Shadow Magic Gems
‡ 1 Light Magic Gem	

Monsters

‡ Chupacabras	‡ Cave Troll
‡ Headless Burrower	‡ Small Troll

Unlockable Trial

‡ Finish the level after killing ten Headless Corpses, without being grabbed by them a single time

Walkthrough

Gabriel's Wings

This level helps you get used to the new powers of the relic that you acquired at the end of the previous level. With the Seraph Shoulders, you can now perform a double jump in midair, which you can also use as an attack movement during certain combos.

As you walk off the initial steps of the portal in the beginning of the level, head toward the camera. Follow the beaten path in the dirt to the left corner to find a dead knight with a **Shadow Magic Gem**. On the opposite path, a Neutral Elemental Fountain can be found. And a Health Font is located where the paths meet behind the portal.

Find the dead Brotherhood knight in the small brick enclosure directly behind and attached to the entry portal. This knight holds a **Light Magic Gem**.

In the dead end with the old wooden rowboat, find a vertical wall with Grip ledges. To reach the first Grip ledge, double jump using the Seraph Shoulders to reach the high ledge.

By double jumping from the small bump on the ground, you can reach the safe ledge above. From there, move left and jump at the edge toward the platform. You can now double jump again to reach a path, in the level above.

After a short clear path, you find another obstacle: a large hole in the ground. You can jump down without dying, but won't be able to continue; you must jump over it using the magic shoulders. If you combine the sprint with the double jump, you can get through a large gap in a single jump. If you miss the jump and get to the small platform below, you can use a double jump to get to the ledge above.

Headless Burrowers

Just beyond the sprint and double jump pit, you'll get to a camp where a new enemy is presented: the Headless Burrowers, or what we like to refer to as "zombies." Once you see them in action, you'll realize the name says it all. They burrow underground and throw their heads at you when surfaced.

Your primary objective is to destroy the corpses, as they keep generating more heads unless stopped. To make them emerge from the ground, you have to destroy all the current floating heads to make the corpses come up to replenish them. It is during this process that they are vulnerable.

Once you have destroyed the headless corpses, a wall of tiki-looking statues is destroyed, revealing a path branching off to the right from this camp. There's also a pathway leading out of the camp on the left side. The path on the right can wait, as you'll need to travel that way later.

Left Route from Headless Burrowers' Camp

Along the left route from the headless camp, you find another bottomless pit; this time, you must sprint out over the pit and then wait a moment before performing the second jump to land at the cave entrance at a lower level. If instead you jump across the gap to the other side, you find more headless corpses.

You must learn how to maximize vertical and horizontal displacement when double jumping; the trajectory can be very different depending on the exact moment when you press the Jump button a second time.

SECRET CAMP: SHADOW MAGIC GEM

If you jump the second pit and land on the pathway above the tunnel entrance, then you'll discover a camp with a dead knight holding a **Shadow Magic Gem**. Tiki statues block your passage, forcing you to finish off the Headless Burrowers to exit.

The small underground cave ends at an extra long gorge where you must sprint and double jump to then reach a Grip Point with your chain (all in one big glorious move).

Continue this jump by swinging out as far as you can with the chain and then performing another double jump to hook the second Grip Point in the gorge. The third and last jump ends with a ledge grab. Pull yourself up to the continuing pathway and the beginning of another cinematic.

Return of the Chupacabras

Just when you were falling in love with your new rune, a darn Chupacabras takes your powers and vanishes! The Chupacabras hides in the Troll Cave (right path from the Headless Burrowers' camp). However, to get back there, you should have to use your missing relics (especially the magic shoulders), so you must find a new path.

Luckily, there is a secondary entrance to the cave just before the point where the Chupacabras appeared: you can find a climbable wall on the right side of the path.

To the right of your position when the Chupacabras steals your relics, you'll find a Grip ledge and a dead knight on a wooden platform. Take the **Life Magic Gem** from the knight and continue up to the top of the hill. Enter the cave and do battle with the Cave Troll.

Do not kill the Cave Troll. Instead, tame it and mount it. You need the Cave Troll to destroy the large boulder blocking the other half of the cave. Once you've broken through the boulder, enter the next cave through the unblocked hole.

Defeat the smaller Trolls in the next cave and then destroy the glowing boulder to reveal the Chupacabras. Choke and dismount the Cave Troll, and then grab the little thief and retrieve your stolen runes.

Take the **Scroll** from the Brotherhood knight on the ledge that leads to the first Headless Burrowers' camp. Head back into the cave and leave using the same route you used to enter. At the bottom of the hill where the Chupacabras stole your runes, you'll find a path through the burning woods. Head that way now.

Sprint and double jump along the left edge of the next gorge to land on a remaining piece of the path near a burning building. Jump to the next ledge beside the burning structure, and the ledge soon gives way. As you fall, you'll see a Grip Point in the gorge below. Use the Hook Tip to grapple to a lower ledge on the right side of the ravine.

Run off the far side of the ledge and latch onto a Grip ledge further ahead in the ravine. Shimmy around the corner and backwards jump to the wooden frame behind you. Use this framework to reach another ledge you can put your feet on.

Sprint out of the following tunnel exit and perform a double jump at the crest of your jump to reach the high Grip Point with your Hook Tip. Swing to the glowing Grip ledge and hang on with your hands. Finish climbing out of the pit using the Grip ledges, shimmying, and double jumps.

Find a knight on the exit path. He holds a Scroll describing the spotting of Gandolfi and goes on to speak of a weapon of his that will surely save us all.

LEVEL TWO: WOES MOOR

The stench of death is strong. A witch holds power here, but I sense Gabriel is more than a match for her. The bones of his fellow warriors litter the place, but he seems oblivious to them. Stoic and determined to move forward, he doggedly fights on. He has not slept for days, he rests only briefly. I sometimes hear him talking to her, that they will be together again. In the dark, he weeps for her, or perhaps it is for his own lost soul.

Hidden Items

‡ 1 Life Magic Gem   ‡ 1 Shadow Magic Gem
‡ 2 Light Magic Gems

Monsters

‡ Mandragora   ‡ Scarecrow

Unlockable Trial

‡ Finish the level and get the three keys, scaring the crows only 13 times

Walkthrough

The Strawmen and the Crows

After speaking with the witch Baba Yaga, Gabriel has a new mission: he has to find the three keys that open the magical music box in her cottage. However, three evil scarecrows that roam through the abandoned farms guard the keys.

When control returns to you, walk toward the camera along the path that led you to the house in the cinematic. You'll find a dead Brotherhood knight holding a **Shadow Magic Gem**.

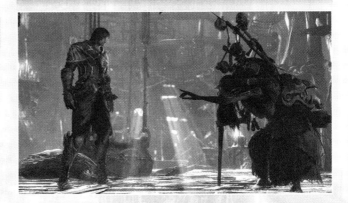

Follow the only path beyond the witch's house, and you'll find another knight in a puddle of water. Take his hint **Scroll**. You can chose to unlock the solution, but there is no need; you have this guide, so keep those solution credits.

Puzzle Solution

The scarecrows are lying around the area, but they won't move until awakened by a flock of birds. In this case, you can use crows to do so. As you start the challenge, you see a device that looks like a driven well, with some crows perched on top of it. Upon closer inspection, the wagon wheel on its side glows, showing that the object is interactive. Use the wagon wheel to shake the structure and send the crows flying in the opposite direction. Use the left stick as indicated to shake the wheel.

CAMERA HELP

While you are using the interactive objects in this puzzle, the camera points toward the next one and, in certain cases, toward a group of two or three posts that the crows might use if scared from the current position. Try to predict the movement of the crows and how you can you lead them to the scarecrows before taking actions.

Activating the first scarecrow is pretty straightforward: just repeat the process at the next well, and the crows fly towards the enemy. Also along the route, a Mandragora soon attacks you.

The First Key

The scarecrow enters the combat area with its scythe arms as weapons. Like other mid-stage bosses, you can only finish it off by completing a Grip finishing move challenge after inflicting enough damage. Once you have dodged attacks and beaten the scarecrow to an inch of its life, the boss starts glowing. Grab the scarecrow and press the indicated button repeatedly to finish it off. The scarecrow leaves a **Key** behind. Pick it up with the Use button.

The Second and Third Keys

Now that you can recognize the scarecrows when they are idle, it's only a matter of finding the way of leading the crows to them. Continue straight through the arena where you fought the first scarecrow. A few meters away, you find the second one. And in this case, the group of crows that you used to awake it won't be enough. The crows follow a branch in the path (defined by the wells) and don't fly towards the enemy. To force them to move in the correct direction, you must block the alternative routes using additional flocks.

There's a ruined windmill at the far end of the second scarecrow area. Pull the boards down with your Spiked Chain to reach this raised platform. You can find a knight with a **Light Magic Gem** on the far end of this platform.

212

Here, you also find the second crow group. Push them forward using the wagon wheel and leave them in the path branch ahead. Now, shaking any of the two wells makes the crows enter the arena with the second scarecrow. Defeat the second scarecrow just as you did the first, and you acquire the second **Key**.

The last of the three scarecrows is a little better hidden than the rest; to wake it, you must use three flocks this time. The concept is the same as in the previous two cases: the crows fly toward the nearest well in the path; if they find it occupied, they fly to the closest post (returning back if they cannot locate a suitable landing place). Make sure to remove the boarded up roofless barn to find the Brotherhood knight holding the **Light Magic Gem**.

Defeat the final scarecrow just as you did the others and acquire the final **Key**. Once all three scarecrows have been defeated and with the keys in your pocket, return to Baba Yaga's hut.

LAST MAGIC GEM

As soon as you defeat the final scarecrow and pick up the last key, pivot to the right and head into the little stable. The camera turns slightly, revealing a glowing Brotherhood knight. This soldier holds the Life Magic Gem.

Take the glowing lift back up to the witch's stilt house. When you deliver the three keys to Baba Yaga, she conjures up a spell that she says can shrink you and fit you into her music box. This ends the level, and hopefully not your life.

Good, good. Now Baba put you inside the box.

LEVEL THREE:
THE MUSIC BOX

The old hag has cast a spell on Gabriel, making him very small. Small enough to enter the music box and retrieve the blue rose she so obviously desires. This old witch has me nervous. Something she said has filled me with disquiet. She mentioned the "King of the Angels"... I am sure I heard her correctly. What does this mean? Why do I have this feeling of dread? I hope Gabriel will succeed and quickly, so that we may be on our way. When he has gone, I will kill this evil crow, so that she may no longer be a danger to anyone else ever again.

Hidden Items

‡ 1 Life Magic Gem   ‡ 1 Light Magic Gem

Unlockable Trial

‡ Finish the level and get the blue rose without falling in any of the music box traps

Walkthrough

Music Box Mk III

Baba Yaga's magic spell has teleported you inside the small music box. You can actually see her watching your progress across the labyrinth while you solve the puzzle. After the cutscene, you find yourself in the music box near a strange glowing device in one of the walls. To interact with it, first you need to get the first music cylinder, which is located in the middle of the same room.

Green Cylinder

With the Green Cylinder in your hands (displayed in the top right corner once in your possession), you can now use the nearby music machine puzzle. It controls the activation of the traps around the area by using music. While one of the cylinders is being played, the traps in one or more of the passageways stop, allowing you to cross them safely. The moment you use the music machine, a hint **Scroll** enters your Travel Book automatically.

When the play button in the machine is pressed, all of the inserted cylinders start being played in turns, so when one part stops, the next one starts. To cross the labyrinth, you must discover the correct order of the various cylinders to open the traps that lead to the goal. However, this is not an easy task, as all the music cylinders are scattered around the music box, behind passages filled with deadly traps.

PUZZLE CONTROLS

Use the left stick to move the selection marker across the puzzle. Press the Jump button to highlight a cylinder or switch places with the selected one. Select the play button (the rightmost button) and press Jump to start the music.

CARPET COLORS

The carpet colors in each passageway match the color of the music cylinder that stops the trap within it. Explore your surroundings before moving to avoid unnecessary backtracking!

The following is the association of traps and colors:

Cylinder	Type of Trap	Details
Green	Spikes trap	Use the sprint to cross once the spikes retract.
Red	Platforms trap	Jump (try not to use double jump, or you will fall past the platform) to the next platform as soon as it rises.
Magenta	Blades trap	Use a dodge movement to cross beneath one of the blade traps, and double jump to pass above the other one.
Yellow	Fire trap	Study the timing of the fire movements and jump on the empty spaces (try not to use double jump, or you might fall in the middle of a fire wave).
Blue	Electric trap	Run forward in the first half of the trap and double jump over the second one.

Puzzle Solution

The hint Scroll says, "The blue rose is on the other side of the box. To reach it, use the following sequence of music cylinders: **Red, Blue, Magenta,** and **Green**." This is the step-by-step solution to the puzzle:

Take the **Green Cylinder**, in the starting room, and use the device next to it to cross the green spikes trap and get the **Red Cylinder**. Notice the Brotherhood knight in the middle of the green hazard hallway. If you stop to get the **Light Magic Gem**, you may get killed, but you retain the gem and just have to race through on your next pass.

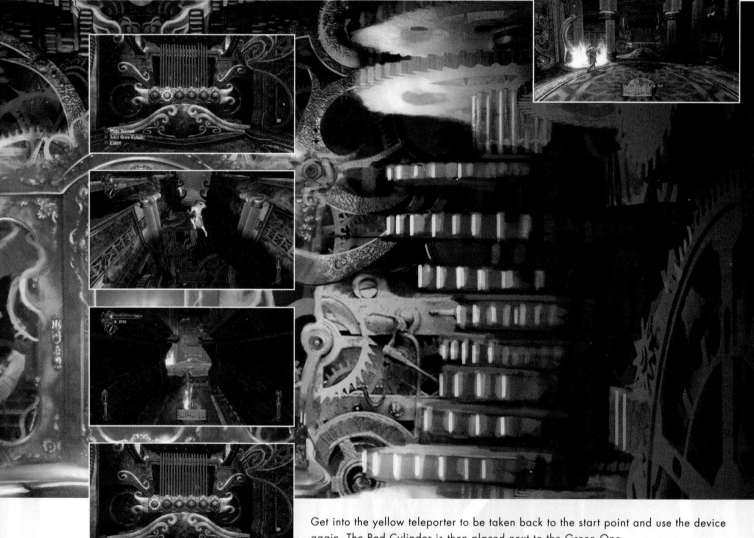

Get into the yellow teleporter to be taken back to the start point and use the device again. The Red Cylinder is then placed next to the Green One.

Switch the **Red** and **Green Cylinders** and activate the machine again.

Cross the red platform trap, and in the next room, head left towards the green spikes trap. After the Red Cylinder finishes playing, the green one starts, allowing you to cross the green spikes trap and get the **Magenta Cylinder**. Use the teleporter to return to start.

Insert the new cylinder in the machine and activate it again; this time in this order: **Red, Magenta, Green**. This allows you to obtain the **Yellow Cylinder.**

Teleport back to the start and use the machine again starting with **Red** and **Yellow** first and then the other two used in any order. In the second room, turn left to cross the yellow firetrap and get the last cylinder—the **Blue**.

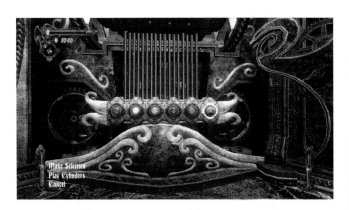

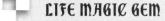

LIFE MAGIC GEM

The next time you return to the chamber where you found the Blue Cylinder, there will be a dead knight in its place. This knight holds the Life Magic Gem.

With all five music cylinders in the machine, the final combination to get to the room of the **Blue Rose** is: **Red, Blue, Magenta,** and **Green.**

As soon as you get the blue rose, Baba Yaga casts a new spell to get you outside again. In exchange for the flower, she teleports you to the necromancer lands.

CHAPTER X

LEVEL ONE: TITAN GRAVEYARD

Baba Yaga sent our hero to the titans' Graveyard and I have sent her soul to the underworld. She will trouble us no more. Now my friend enters the Land of the Dead and his final battle is coming. I must find my own path and try to meet with him at some point. For now he is on his own. The land requires sacrifice…a sacrifice I hope that he can make, because without it he will not get very far. I must have faith in him now. The seed was sown long ago and it flowers beautifully. He has come this far down the path…I must believe that he will go all the way.

Hidden Items

‡ 1 Life Magic Gem ‡ 1 Shadow Magic Gem
‡ 2 Light Magic Gems

Monsters

‡ Creeping Coffin ‡ Skeleton Warrior
‡ Creeping Corpse

Unlockable Trial

‡ Finish the level after receiving at least 100 points of poison damage from the deadly mist

Walkthrough

Deadly Mist

The teleportation spell has left you in the lands of the necromancer. You start the level in a strange structure made up of crystals, which happens to be the interior of a colossus.

Climbing out of the titan, you overlook an ominous battleground. Here, the titans of the wizards, made their last charge against the Dark Lords centuries ago. Now, only mechanical corpses remain—mountainous ghosts in the haze.

Throughout this level, like some previously visited, a deadly mist envelops the ground in certain places. You will only last a couple seconds in the poison before dying, so try to avoid it. Grapple and climb down the chest of the decaying colossus.

When you touch down in the area below the colossus, you stand in a large arena surrounded by a fog. A dead Brotherhood Knight lies in eternal slumber on the right side of the area. He holds a **Scroll** that says only those with corruption in their heart are able to gain access to the Land of the Dead.

Use a Sprint and a double jump to cross the narrowest pool of poison from the first landing area to the titan's kneecap. Repeat this jumping maneuver to reach the next area of safety.

Immediately, some Creeping Corpses and two Skeleton Warriors attack you. Holy Water does wonders on these undead creatures. After dealing with them, find another Brotherhood Knight corpse in the sunlight under the limb of an old colossus. He has a **Scroll** that suggests using Shadow Magic to pass for becoming "evil".

Climb up the downed titan on your left and walk along its chest until you see a large hole in its ribcage. Drop down to get a **Light Magic Gem,** then use double jump to use the Grip ledge to get back out.

Turn back the way you came and Sprint and double jump to the titan's kneecap. Turn towards the titan to your right; sprint and double jump to the ledge at the base of the upraised titan arm.

Run up the arm, then sprint and double jump off the end of the most extended finger to clear the wide gap and reach the next platform.

Creeping Coffin

As soon as you land on the titan's back a new enemy type appears: the Creeping Coffin. These parasitic creatures emerge through small fractures in the titan's stone body and quickly enter an empty sarcophagus.

The easiest way to deal with these enemies is to prevent them from entering a sarcophagus. If they make it into a coffin they will use it as armor, gaining health and damage resistance. In this new combat area, notice the broken circular rune: identical to the ones you had to destroy while fighting the ice and stone colossi. Your task is to find the missing stone piece and complete the rune to power the titan again.

After smashing all the coffins around the area and annihilating all the creepers, defeat the last corpse in a coffin using a Grab challenge to jump into the coffin and throw the corpse out. This breaks the coffin making it impossible for the creeper to crawl back in. Defeat the Creeping Corpse and grab the **Rune Fragment** after the battle is won.

LIFE MAGIC GEM

Before using the rune, climb the titan's left arm to reach a stone platform where a **Life Magic Gem** can be obtained from a dead Brotherhood Knight.

Use the rune on the keyhole and in a short cutscene, the titan will reanimate and in a last desperate effort to reach the necromancer fortress, it will move its left arm forward toward the black wall. The colossus' last movement allows you to reach the next area in the mist by traveling along its arm. From the extended hand, sprint and double jump towards the clear sandy island and the first checkpoint.

Inside the Colossus

From this island you can reach two different titans. First, you need to head for the titan on the right (you need rune keys to proceed on the left titan). Use Sprint and double jump to reach the platform.

TITAN ON THE RIGHT

While on the first ledge, double jump to the outer platform to the right to find a knight **Scroll** and a bag of daggers.

Return to the first ledge and enter the tunnel (heading away from the camera). Continue into, what seems like a shallow second cave. Once inside, turn sharply to the right to discover an opening.

Inside the body of the titan, you are attacked again by Creeping Corpses trying desperately to become Creeping Coffins; like in the prior encounter, one of them holds the rune key that you need to continue. Destroy all the coffins first. Once you destroy all the enemies, grab the **Rune Fragment** and head back to the sandy island. Equipped with the rune, head to titan on the left.

TITAN ON THE LEFT

When you reach the titan on the left, head to the back ledge (which is actually the front of the titan) and find the **Shadow Magic Gem** on the dead knight below the titan's chest.

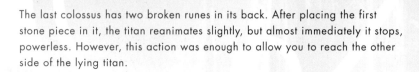

The last colossus has two broken runes in its back. After placing the first stone piece in it, the titan reanimates slightly, but almost immediately it stops, powerless. However, this action was enough to allow you to reach the other side of the lying titan.

Head to the front of the titan and use the ledges in its armpit to reach the newly extended arm. Sprint and double jump off the end of its raised hand to clear the poison swamp.

In the new area, more Creeping Corpses attack. One of the enemies from this group holds the last **Rune Fragment** that you need to finish the level.

Find the **Light Magic Gem** on the dead knight under the hand of the titan where the latest fight occurs with the Creeping Corpses.

After you finally acquire the rune from winning the corpse battle, jump up to the ledge and travel across the titan's arm. Double jump back the way you came, then head to the titan's back to insert the fragment into the second incomplete rune. With its power source back again, the titan tries to complete the movement it started earlier.

Pass back under its arm. You will battle a Skeleton Warrior and a few Creeping Corpses. After defeating the enemies, Grip climb the titan's spine to reach its shoulder. Run along its extended arm and jump from the end of its hand to the round platform below in the swamp to complete the level.

LEVEL TWO: FIRE PINNACLE

Powerful Necromancers have used this once sacred ground to build an army of the dead. Conquering nearby lands, legions of Zombies have devoured the living and given rise to this desolation. No man has travelled here without meeting death. Gabriel now faces his toughest challenge. He now bangs his fists on the very doors of hell on Earth and the Lord who commands here is listening, waiting for him. Smiling…

But one path must end here.

Monsters

‡ The Silver Warrior

Unlockable Trial

‡ Finish the level without allowing Pan to recover any health during the fight

Boss Battle:
The Silver Warrior

Finally, you have arrived at the necromancer fortress and stand before the dreaded passage. It is here you reencounter Pan. The faun tests your abilities one last time, in a "training" fight that determines who will be sacrificed for the greater good. In a cutscene, Pan shape-shifts into a mighty warrior, clad in silver armor. Just before the battle begins, the Silver Warrior strips you of all magic to see how you do without this luxury.

Stage One

In this non-magical state, its best to lower the Silver Warrior's health using standard combo attacks. Use rolling dodges to pass under his low chain swipes. A good rule of thumb is to roll dodge, use a combo attack, then roll dodge, and so on. The key is to issue damage and stay as safe as possible.

SIT ON DEFENSE

In this stage, don't fight too offensively; the lack of light magic means that you won't be able to recover your health, so it's better to try a defensive approach.

Once his health is about a quarter depleted, he becomes stunned for a short time, glowing to the point that you can grab him. Beat the halo and button press challenges during this segment to throw him to the ground and twist his arm. This returns the Light Magic ability to you.

Stage Two

Now both characters can use Light magic abilities. In this, and the next stage, a new fighting concept is presented: attacks made with identical magic type used cause less damage (and do more damage if opposite magic is being used). The key to quickly deplete the enemy's health while conserving yours is to turn off Light Magic when the Silver Warrior is also using Light Magic. You will do more damage. So only turn it on when you need to recover health.

The boss's health meter turns invincible grey when you knock him down to about half of his health remaining. Use a Grab to begin up the halo ring challenge. The first button press causes you to punch the Silver Warrior in the gut. The next hit is a punch to the jaw. The third hit knocks the boss back down when he tries to recover from the previous hit. Completing this challenge returns your Shadow Magic.

Stage Three

Now both opponents are able to use their Light and Shadow Magic powers. Remember to switch magic types as fast as you can, to attack the Silver Warrior with the opposite magic that he is using at any given time. When the boss throws back its arms be prepared to dodge one of its projections: Pan the horse and Pan the eagle. Jump over or roll dodge to avoid these attacks.

The stage ends with Pan leaving the combat arena to throw his boomerang blade at you from a higher position. To finally kill the faun, you have to use this boomerang against him: you have to successfully dodge the spinning blade while you are near him (halo ring challenge). If done correctly, the weapon hits Pan, ending the fight. If you fail, the Silver Warrior regains some health and you must beat him back down to this ending sequence again.

LEVEL THREE: FIRE CEMETERY

So the old god is dead. It has come to this, at the last. The blood of a god has opened the way. Good Gabriel, very good. There is only one true God and all usurpers must be cast aside. Though Pan's sacrifice was not in vain. Now our warrior of light can proceed to his final destiny. The Lord of the Dead is the most powerful of the Lords of Shadow. Gabriel will need every ounce of his being to defeat him. I worry for him though, his mind is tired, broken even. He questions his faith, he questions his heart. Can he succeed? Come my friend, just a bit further and you shall see your Marie again.

Hidden Items	
‡ 2 Life Magic Gems	‡ 1 Light Magic Gem

Monsters	
‡ Chupacabras	‡ Zombie

Unlockable Trial

‡ Finish the level after killing 20 Zombies is a single aerial sequence

Walkthrough

Meet the Horde

Pan's sacrifice has opened the gate to the necromancer fortress. The first area you have to cross is the graveyard; this area is the habitat of the Zombie horde.

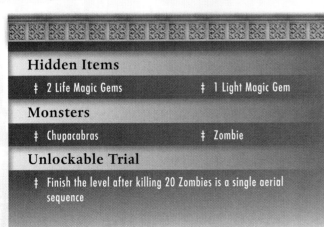

Continue through the deep gorge using double jumps, Grip ledges, shimmying and backward jumps to make it to a distant ledge on the right side of the canyon where you do battle with the first of the Zombie hordes. Walk towards the camera on the battle ledge to find a bag of daggers. Zombies hate daggers.

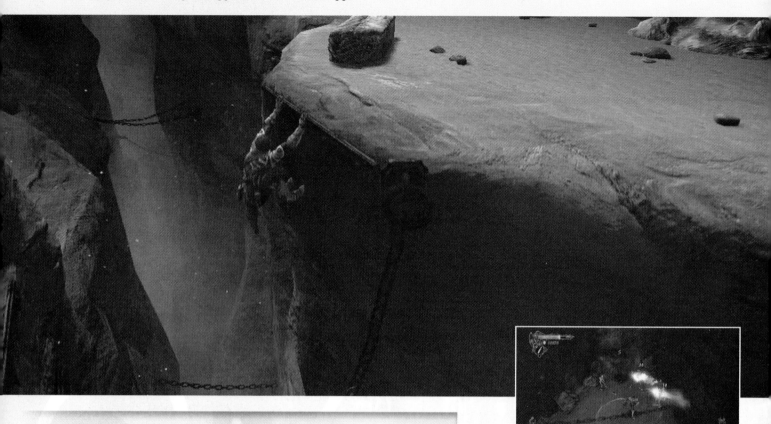

DIVIDE AND CONQUER

Zombies are really weak and won't stand more than one or two hits before crumbling in a pile of ash and bones. However, being surrounded by a horde of them will get you killed, so don't try to rush through the level.

Just beyond the first Zombie encounter you reach a split in the path. The left fork continues through the gorge, while the right fork takes you to a **Light Magic Gem**. Take the right fork and jump down into large hole where you battle Zombies. After defeating the Zombies, use a double jump and Grip the ledges in the back right corner to reach the dead Brotherhood Knight. He holds a **Light Magic Gem**.

Back at the canyon fork, drop off the left side of the cliff and use a series of hand holds along the right canyon wall. Stay ahead of the collapsing ledges behind you. The last ledge forces you to jump backwards and latch onto a Grip Point with the Hook Tip in midair. Climb down the chain until you reach the low ledge on the left side. Follow this pathway into a large clearing.

Ravine

Use the Health Font at the entrance to the new area. This next part is a bit tricky. Perform a regular jump off the edge of the ravine. As your head drops below the distant Grip Point on the next ledge, perform a double jump. The Grip Point becomes active as you begin to fall after the double jump. Use the Hook Tip to latch onto it, then climb to the top of the ledge.

Chupacabra Trouble

As soon as you reach the new pathway across the ravine a mischievous Chupacabra takes your relics, leaving you without magic powers again.

The Chupacabra quickly teleports to a large, cage-like structure that seems impossible to breach. There are three stone heads on top of the "cage". Each one of these heads has glowing, purple eyes. To open the cage you have to direct the light towards each of the heads. To achieve this, you use light emitting statues like the ones found in the Lycanthrope and Vampire levels.

First, begin your approach to the Chupacabra and you'll come across a dead Brotherhood Knight with a hint **Scroll**. Use our guide instead of accepting the answer to the puzzle so you don't lose points. The Scroll says: each lock opens only after being hit by a light ray coming from one of the monoliths. To cast the beam, these floating stones must be powered by a completed crystal. Despite the stones' size, they can be moved by hitting them with a melee weapon. However, their movement is restricted to the glowing rails in the ground. If you happen to have only one power crystal, you can reuse it in the different monoliths.

Exploring the area, you can find a dead knight holding a **Life Magic Gem** at the "bottom" (toward the camera position) of the area. The knight lies on the ground near the fiery ravine.

Toward the bottom middle of the area, near a small, round fire fissure, you can find the final collectible on a dead Brotherhood Knight tucked in a small earthen nook: a **Life Magic Gem**.

Solving Chupacabra Cage Lock Puzzle

To make things easier to understand, we'll describe the terminology of objects used in this puzzle and the strategy:

GLOSSARY OF TERMS

Item	Description
Lock	One of the three rock face locks around the Chupacabra cage that must be broken with a Dark Crystal light beam to open the cage.
Dark Crystal Device	You insert a Dark Crystal into a fixed device (they glow) and then the energy travels through a connected rail. One of the three Dark Crystal devices is broken and cannot be used, so a workaround is necessary.
Monolith	Floating stones used to generate a light beam that breaks the cage locks. They run on Dark Crystal energy delivered through rails and generated from a Dark Crystal Device. Monoliths move by striking them with a melee weapon (punches are not necessary).
Glowing Rails	Monoliths are moved along rails. These rails only light when a Dark Crystal is inserted in the Dark Crystal Device connected to its rail.

First Lock

First, get a Dark Crystal from the deposit near the floating stone **(A)** and place it in the Dark Crystal Device (**Yellow Circle**) activate the first **Monolith A**. Once activated, the Rail beneath the Monolith glows purple. This Rail marks the path that the Monolith can be pushed. To move a Monolith, simply hit it with a normal melee attack.

Breaking the first lock is pretty simple: knock the Monolith to the far end **(1)** of its Glowing Rail. Once there, rotate it until the light beam hits the first of the heads.

Second Lock

For the second and third locks, you have to make the light beam bounce off more than one Monolith. This is necessary because the connected Dark Crystal Device is broken. Place **Monolith C** to the right end of its rail **(2)**, and **Monolith A** [which is now in position **(1)**] back in its starting position **(A)**. Rotate **Monolith A** to point at the **Monolith C** at **(2)**, then rotate the **Monolith** C at **(2)** to bounce the light beam through the gap in the rocks so it hits the second lock.

Third Lock

For the last lock, you must remove the Dark Crystal from the active Dark Crystal Device **(Yellow Circle)** and then insert it in the other Dark Crystal Device **(Red Circle)**. Afterward, **Monolith B** should be moved to the end of its path **(3)** and rotated so its beam shoots towards the **Monolith C**, which must be repositioned at the left end of its rail **(4)**. From there, the correct rotation of the Monolith makes the light impact the final lock.

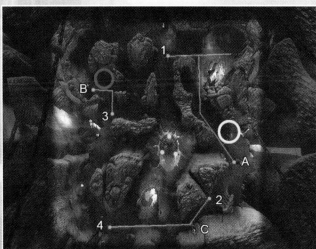

Retrieve Your Relics

Now that the cage has been destroyed, jump up onto the cage platform and grab the Chupacabra to solve the puzzle and to get your relics back.

Gong Puzzle

In front of the crematory where the path ends, you find a Zombie horde and two identical gongs. Defeat the Zombies, then work on the puzzle. You can make the gongs sound by using a Gauntlet Punch: hold the Block button then press the Direct Attack button. Make sure to enable Shadow Magic before punching the gongs.

To open the door to the crematory, you must get both of the gongs sounding at the same time. Punch one of the gongs, dash in the direction of the other and use Gauntlet Punch again before the first one stops ringing. If you run out of Dark Magic energy to perform a dash, try dodge rolling or sprinting. The crematory door opens when the puzzle is solved. Enter the crematory to complete the level.

LEVEL FOUR: CREMATORY OVEN

Fueled by the very flames of hell itself, the crematory oven is where the Gravedigger does his ghastly work. He is a powerful demon whose mighty shovel can cleave a man in two with one stroke. The Gravedigger will rip the very soul from Gabriel, given half the chance, yet I sense that our hero is more than a match for this creature. This could be interesting indeed. I sense Gabriel's rage welling up within him and I wonder who is the more terrible, our hero or the demon?

Hidden Items

‡ 1 Shadow Magic Gem

Monsters

‡ Creeping Coffin   ‡ Gravedigger

‡ Creeping Corpse

Unlockable Trial

‡ Finish the level and kill at least 15 summoned creeping corpses during the light against the Gravedigger

Boss Battle: Gravedigger

You've reached the crematory. This is where the Gravedigger works and lives. You'll catch a glimpse of him the moment you enter, but he leaves before you can take a closer look. He summons several Creeping Corpses to occupy you. He also closes the door, trapping you in with the monsters.

Defeat the Creeping Corpses before they can enter the coffins conveniently lying around. There's another wave of Creeping Corpses to attack, so be sure that all coffins are destroyed before you take out the Creeping Coffin so that enemies in the next wave have no where to escape.

After you defeat all the enemies, the door opens, giving you a clear path to the Gravedigger. Before you enter the arena, fill up on magic and health using the fountains on either side of the arena entrance.

Stage One

When you are about to enter the arena, the ground breaks behind you preventing you from exiting the arena. The Gravedigger is tough; during the combat, it uses a shovel to unearth more Creeping Corpses and discharges shockwaves causing different ground sections to collapse. The shovel also sends out fire that runs along the ground and should be avoided.

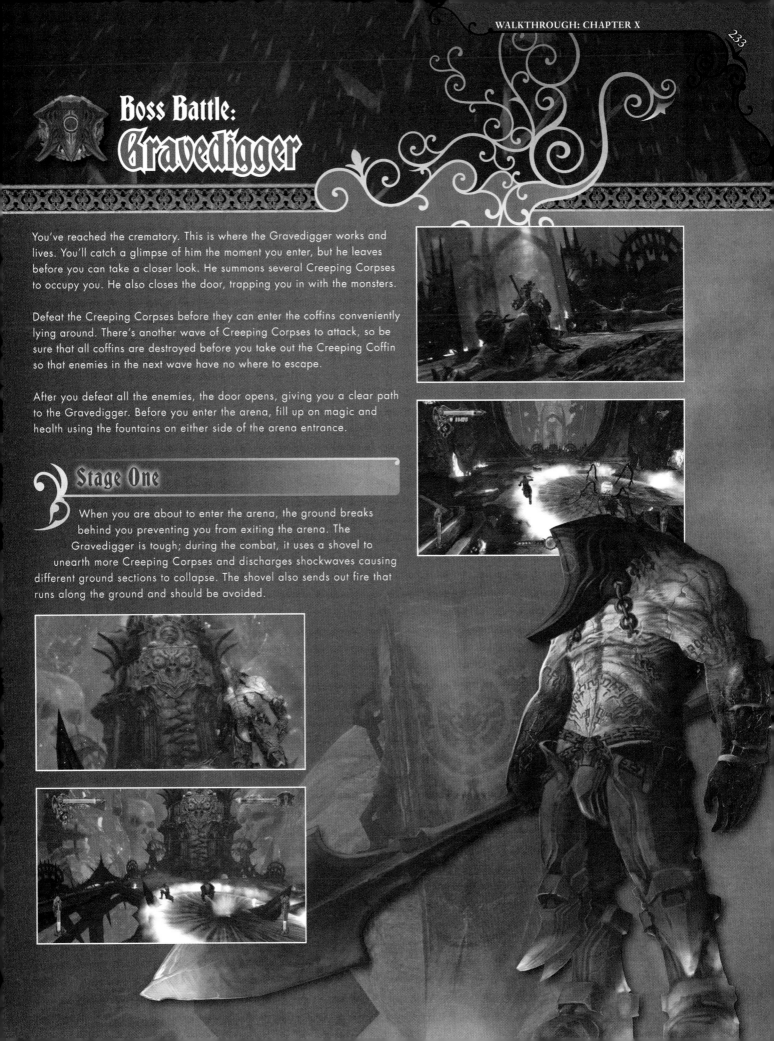

The boss swipes and swings his shovel like a sword and expels long tentacles from its mouth, an attack similar to the Creeping Corpses'.

Use Shadow Magic to increase the damage of your melee attacks. Roll dodge to avoid the melee attacks and double jump to avoid the shockwave attacks. Creeping Corpses are summoned about halfway through Gravedigger's health meter. Attempt to use wide-reaching attacks that include the boss while concentrating on getting rid of the regular enemies quickly.

Stage Two

When you knock the Gravedigger's health down to about 10% remaining (when the meter turns invincible gray), the boss becomes stunned and begins to glow, indicating you can now grab him. Instead of grabbing and attacking him, which will get you nowhere, move to the right side of the central oven and *Use* the Stake in the glowing gear mechanism.

Complete the four halo ring challenges to successfully crank the door open until it stays open. There is plenty of time to do this while the boss remains stunned. In fact, there's enough time to crank the doors open and jump on Gravedigger's back (press the Use button). The final struggle over his mighty shovel begins. There are no halo challenges, simply press the indicated buttons repeatedly when they appear on two separate occasions.

The end result has you knocking the Gravedigger into the deep furnace. Just when you think it's over, his tentacles appear from the depths, grabs onto you and attempt to pull you to a fiery end. Press any button when the halo challenge appears to escape a fiery fate by grabbing onto another ledge. You manage to pry the tentacles off you and, fortunately, grip onto a narrow earthen bridge before plummeting into the lava pit.

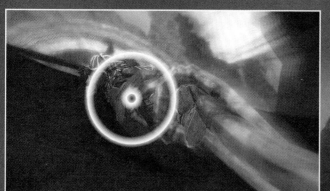

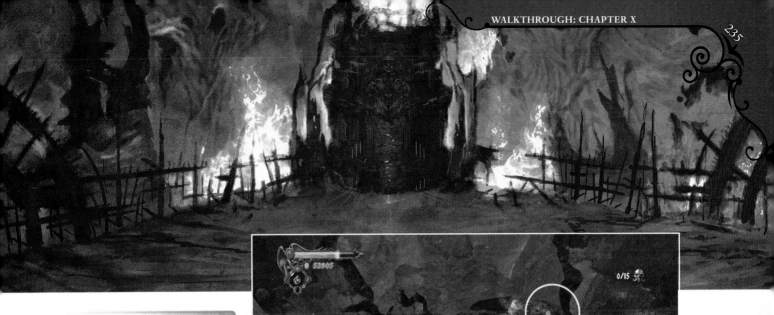

Fried in Lava

The level of the lava beneath you is rising quickly, so you have to exit the level before it gets you. This last part of the level is a race against time, or more precisely, against the lava. The flow keeps increasing over time, so you have to figure out the path upwards, moving faster than the lava. It is not a tough challenge, but you will die if remain still for a few seconds.

After the third Hook Tip use, you climb up the chain and reach a long narrow rim that encircles the entire oven; this can be used as a Grip ledge and just above the Grip Point location are a few ledges sticking out of a crack in the oven. That is the way out of the oven. However, if you want to get the Magic Gem, you must shimmy to the right along this rim until you reach another set of similar ledges. Climb to the top of these to a short ledge where a Brotherhood Knight lies dead. He holds a **Shadow Magic Gem**.

Head back down the way you came and climb up the Grip Ledges to the left above the Grip ring. The camera switches to an external view as you stand on top of the rim of the crematory. Double jump up to another ledge to reach the top of the next level. Use the high Grip Point grapple to a tall spire.

Shimmy around the left corner of the spire where you find a few Grip ledges up higher to hand jump up until you find a high Grip Point on the outer canyon wall. Hook to it and climb the chain to the top to complete the level.

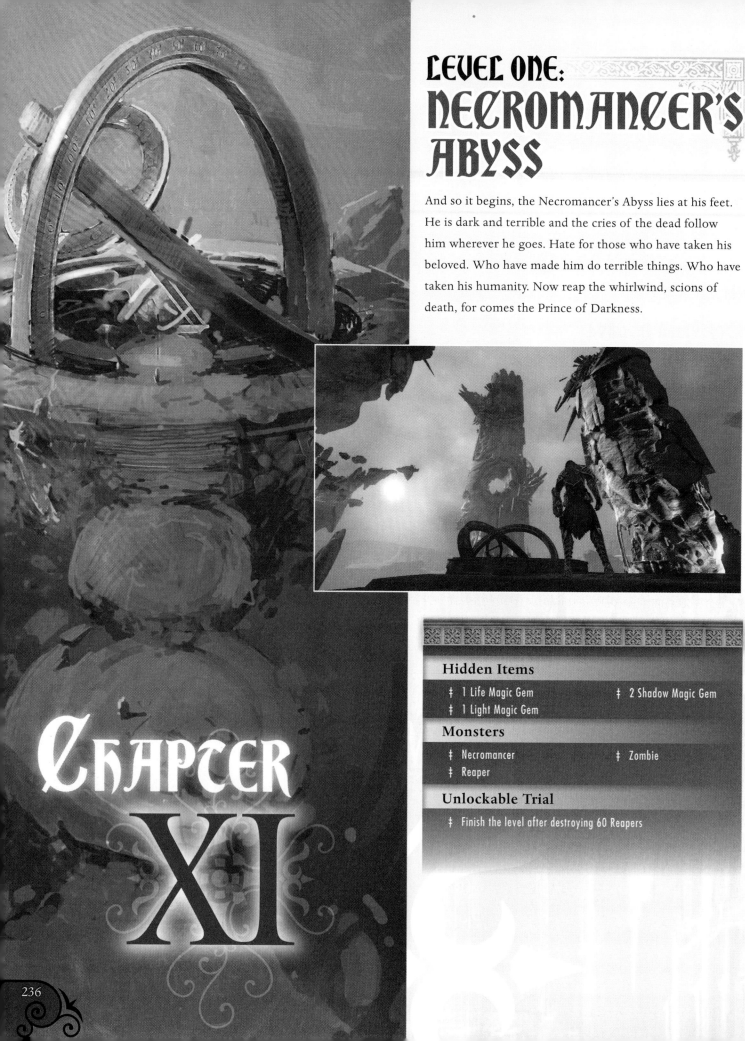

LEVEL ONE: NECROMANCER'S ABYSS

And so it begins, the Necromancer's Abyss lies at his feet. He is dark and terrible and the cries of the dead follow him wherever he goes. Hate for those who have taken his beloved. Who have made him do terrible things. Who have taken his humanity. Now reap the whirlwind, scions of death, for comes the Prince of Darkness.

Hidden Items

‡ 1 Life Magic Gem   ‡ 2 Shadow Magic Gem
‡ 1 Light Magic Gem

Monsters

‡ Necromancer   ‡ Zombie
‡ Reaper

Unlockable Trial

‡ Finish the level after destroying 60 Reapers

CHAPTER XI

Walkthrough

Day of the Eclipse

Gabriel is finally at the heart of the Necromancer Fortress. Three enormous towers float ominously over the abyss. At the very top of each one of them a Necromancer awaits you.

Entering the first tower won't be easy; two puzzles must be solved in order to gain access. You can find the first puzzle right in the beginning of the level, in the middle of the path at the top of the stairs. Find the dead Brotherhood Knight with the hint **Scroll** on right side of the puzzle platform.

Zodiac Puzzle

This large gyroscope is the key to solve the puzzle: the device can alter the position of the sun and the moon in the sky; you have to set them up so there is an eclipse. Move the left stick left or right to select one of the dials (months/days/hours), and up and down to modify its value. Press the Jump button to activate the mechanism.

The correct date is: **8/24/16** (August 24, 4:00 p.m.).

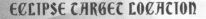

ECLIPSE TARGET LOCATION

There is a single point where an eclipse can occur: right in the middle of the central tower, so it remains visible through the hole. This should make finding the correct date much easier.

After solving this puzzle, some of the surrounding floating rocks merge together to form a single platform. Before you leave the first puzzle platform, explore the ledges on the left side. Jump down to a lower ledge and you can find a dead Brotherhood Knight holding a **Shadow Magic Gem**.

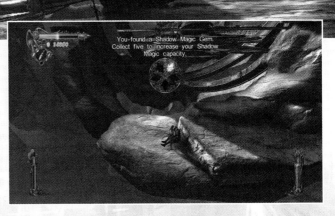

Now leave the platform by traveling along the bridge of boulders that is built as you run across. This is located in the back right corner of the first puzzle platform. When you reach the next platform, the next puzzle presents itself.

Colors are Movements

The dead knight on the right side of this platform holds a hint **Scroll** that reveals the answer to this puzzle. The colored tiles in the ground correspond to different movements of a magic ray of light that moves though the circular door in the front. The system works as follows: you can Earthquake Punch up to eleven tiles and the light ray moves sequentially across the door following the order of the highlighted tiles. Earthquake punch the center tile to input your final sequence.

After a couple attempts of trying to solve the puzzle, it become obvious that each one of the rune colors sends the magic light in a different direction. Starting from outside, the directions associated with each level are: **Up**, **Right**, **Left** and **Down**.

Portals

The portals on this level are different from those found previously: they preserve your speed and momentum upon entrance to the exit point. So for example, if you enter a portal while running, you will exit while still running in the same direction. This mechanic works with all of Gabriel's moves.

Get close to the edge of the platform to get a better view of the path that the light must follow to get all the way up to the top. The camera zooms on the door, giving you a full view of the path embossed on its surface. Complete sequence: **Up, Right, Up, Up, Left, Down, Left, Up, Up, Right, Up.** Remember to ground punch the center tile to complete the challenge.

Once the puzzle door is destroyed you can jump off and double jump onto the next ledge through the gateway. You are on the tower on the right of the crater. Pass through the portal on the next pathway to enter the next platform behind the portal.

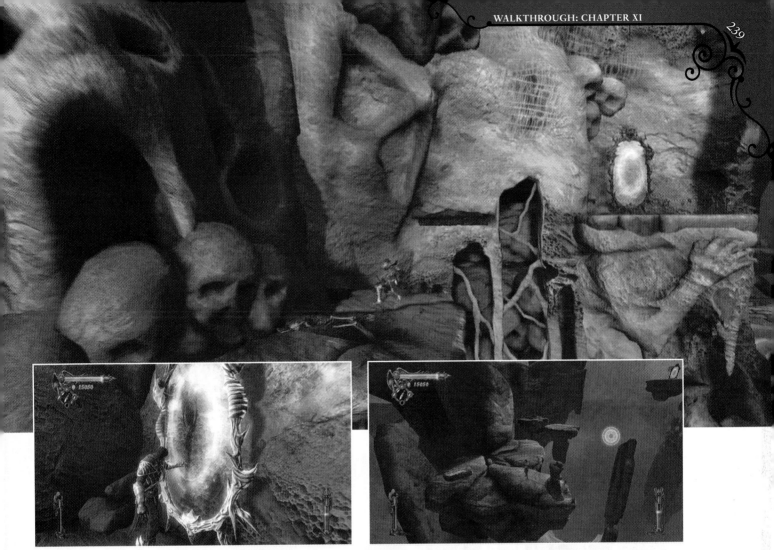

Portal Tower

There are two new portals in the next area as well as a group of Reapers. Defeat the Reapers and explore the ledges on the edge of the ledge heading toward the camera. Here you can find a dead Brotherhood Knight with a **Life Magic Gem**.

To get to the exit on the ledge closest to the entry point you must run into the portal on the ground on the left side of the platform. This way, when you exit in midair you can perform a double jump and reach the ledge above the lower portal. From there, you can double jump to the exit ledge.

Press the Use button while standing next to the exit portal. This teleports you to a floating platform at a halfway point to the tower on the left of the abyss. The path continues through a series of floating moving platforms. Jump from one to the next closest one as it moves toward your current platform. At the top of the next rock spire you'll have to battle a large team of Reapers. Combine the sprint (double tap the left stick) and the double jump to safely reach the next platform.

The next portal found is at the end of the floating rock platforms. It'll leave you to a platform where you'll encounter the first of the necromancers.

Boss Battle:
Necromancer

The Necromancers are a bit different from other bosses: instead of a conventional health bar, their resistance is measured with "Necrotic energy." They use this energy to perform their special attacks.

You can deplete this energy either by attacking the Necromancers directly, or by forcing them to waste it on summon attacks. To achieve that you must try to destroy any creature summoned before they decide to dismiss it to regain the energy spent. In the case of this Necromancer, the boss summons Zombies. It often summons two hordes at once. If you defeat them, then you've taken a lot of health from the boss. If you fail to defeat them before the boss takes them back, then the boss regains the energy used to summon them.

Using the Dark Crystal to summon the Demon from the Shadow Plane works great on the Necromancers, taking a quarter of their health with one summon.

After all their energy is exhausted and the energy bar turns invincible gray, the Necromancer becomes stunned for a short time while they recover and prepare for the next round. You must use that time to perform a Grab movement on them, thus ending the fight.

The grip sequence has two button challenge stages. For the first one, you struggle for the scythe by repeatedly press the onscreen displayed button, then press the next button while the halo glows to run the creature through with his own weapon.

Another One Bites The Dust

TWO PORTALS

After the demise of the first Necromancer, two new portals become accessible on your platform; enter the one on the right to be teleported to a new area where more portals wait.

RIGHT PORTAL: WARP ONE

The next portal platform challenge is trickier: it connects with a location containing another puzzle of gateways. After you exit the portal from the Necromancer battle, you'll see another portal on the right in front of you. You can enter it to teleport above, but you fall down again unless you use your double jump in mid-air to reach the higher teleport mirror. Take this new teleport mirror to the new area.

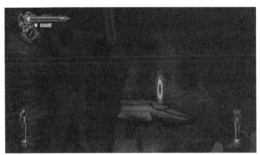

LIGHT MAGIC GEM

To obtain a magic gem from this area, enter the low portal on the left by sprinting and double jumping to the ledge adjacent to it. Jump from the ledge into the portal and double jump when you materialize above it. Use the Hook Tip to attach to the Grip Point on the right wall. Climb to the top of the chain, wall jump and double jump to the ledge with the dead knight holding the **Light Magic Gem**. Use the portal on the same ledge to return to the lower level.

RIGHT PORTAL: WARP TWO

You won't be using any special movements for the next portal; instead, this one requires precise timing to be completed. It teleports you to an exit located in midair, under which a moving rock platform crosses from time to time. You must enter the portal on your ledge at the correct moment so you can safely land on the platform and not fall down into the lower portal, which just returns you to the previous ledge again.

From there, jump to the next platform on the left where some climbing takes you to another teleporting mirror. Once you arrive at this destination, a small group of Reapers materialize, ready to attack. Deal with them, then head to the new warp area though the teleport mirror on the edge of the platform.

Right Portal: Warp Three/Gauntlet Switch One

Defeat the large team of Reapers in the cave and look for the switch before the next teleport mirror. A text prompt hints that the switch requires the power of the Gauntlet. Perform an Earthquake Punch on it to release its energy, which then is given to a mirror behind the stage of dual mirrors where you battled the last Necromancer.

The teleport mirror takes you back to the place where the first Necromancer fell. This time, take the mirror on the left to find the two missing switches.

LEFT PORTAL: WARP ONE

The last portal has dropped you in a new area. You can head left or right through two different portals. Head to the right portal by sprinting and jumping into the suspended portal.

Double jump as you hit the exit point above it and Hook Tip the Grip Point on the small floating boulder above. If you correctly connect all the movements you can swing out and double jump to the next mirror platform without dropping down to a lower platform where Reapers wait.

LEFT PORTAL: WARP TWO/GAUNTLET SWITCH TWO

The last mirror teleports you to a cave similar to the one where you fought the Reapers and Earthquake Punched the first switch. Punch this switch as well and its energy activates the third mirror on the last Necromancer's platform.

Back in the familiar arena from the first Necromancer's fight, take the mirror on the left again.

LEFT PORTAL: WARP ONE (REVISITED)/ GAUNTLET SWITCH THREE

Once you arrive to the familiar floating platform with two portal options on either side, jump this time to the left rock and grab onto the Grip ledge, shimmy around the corner and drop down to the portal below.

This drops you from an exit on the other side of the boulder where you must double jump to reach a Grip Point, swing left and double jump down to a lower ledge. Defeat the next group of Reapers and find a Grip ledge on the lower left that leads to a bit of climbing, stairs, a Health Font, and the third and last switch. When punched, this switch opens the path to the second Necromancer battle.

Three Portal Platform

The platform where you fought the Necromancer now has an available third portal. Head through the opening between the original two portals and use the third portal in the back.

Boss Battle:
The Second Necromancer

The second Necromancer is tougher than the previous one; this Necromancer uses a couple more attacks than the other (he summons Reapers in addition to Zombies and has a new area attack). If you have it, use Holy Water on the Reapers as soon as they are summoned; it takes them out in one quick shot.

Essentially the fighting tactics are the same as used in the first Necromancer battle: drain its energy, counter its attacks, and perform a grab move while it is stunned. You win the struggle over the scythe and end up killing the boss with its own weapon.

To the Top of the Topmost Tower

The fall of the second Necromancer triggers a new portal; this one takes you to the central tower.

You stand on a platform halfway to the top. There are fewer portals here. This is a climbing, double jumping, and grappling zone. Start with a double jump to the left, to hang on the outcrop. From there, move right and continue upwards until the second Grip Point grapple challenge. The next ledge you can get your feet on is a checkpoint.

From the checkpoint, make your way left and up around the tower until you reach the platform with a glowing Grip Point next to it. Four consecutive Grip Points must be connected to reach a couple portals with one Grip Point between them.

Most of the challenge points in this area must be crossed using a double jump, so watch out and look twice before jumping. After these two obstacles, some more climbing finally takes you to the top, ending with a couple Grip Points that allow you to reach the apex of the tower. On the very top of the tower, sprint and double jump across the large gap, then enter the teleport mirror to one last towering mountain.

Final Mountain

When you pass through the teleport mirror on the mountaintop, you find a Health Font on the landing platform of the final mountain.

If you head to the left end of the ledge you can find a continuing, descending route running in a clockwise direction around the mountain tower. Jump the gaps in the path and find a Brotherhood Knight at the end of the path. He holds a **Shadow Magic Gem**. Now return to the Health Font.

Heading to the right (counterclockwise) up the mountain tower you must use double jumps, Grip ledges, shimmies, and backward wall jumps to reach the top. As soon as you pull yourself up to the top of the mountain the level ends successfully.

LEVEL TWO:
THE DRACOLICH

Look at him, so dark, so beautiful. He has come for his revenge and he shall have it. A killing machine without remorse, without pity. What has happened to you, Gabriel? What have you become? Love has blinded you. You have changed, my friend. Your quest is almost over, the dream is in sight. Now you must face death and you must defeat it. The mask is a powerful device and he who wields it can do anything! Bring back the dead, rule the world, destroy the universe, challenge God himself. You are the one, Gabriel. You are the one!

Monsters

‡ Dracolich Titan   ‡ Zombie

Unlockable Trial

‡ Finish the level and defeat the Dracolich in less than 5 minutes

Boss Battle:
Dracolich Titan

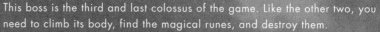

The last Necromancer won't fight like the previous ones; it uses all of its necrotic energy to fuse with a gigantic beast that lies inside the tower, half destroying the tower it in the extraction process. This is the Dracolich, a huge bone dragon almost 600ft long.

This boss is the third and last colossus of the game. Like the other two, you need to climb its body, find the magical runes, and destroy them.

The combat starts with you standing on a platform, and the Dracolich flying around you. The monster sweeps the platform with magic flames each time that crosses it, but you can avoid them by using dodge or dash movements.

You have to wait until the Dracolich passes above you, to use the Hook Tip on the creature's bottom glowing bone spurs. This starts the climbing challenge. While you are waiting for the creature to fly over, you must deal with a horde of Zombies.

Moving along this monster is similar to climbing on the previous colossi. This time, some of the platforms and climbing points are moving. This forces you to carefully adjust the timing of some jumps to avoid falling.

DOUBLE CHECK YOUR GRIP

You can only grab certain parts of the Dracolich
surface. Look for bright zones with bleached bones
exposed to find the correct path.

If you fall, you have the opportunity to save yourself using the Hook Tip
on the edge of the initial platform. This is done by simply passing a single
halo ring challenge. This allows you to continue the battle without having to
restart at a previous checkpoint.

As you work your way up the body of the monster to find the runes, you soon
realize you can only grab onto bones that are lighter in shade and in good
shape; the decayed-looking bones cannot be accessed. When you see a
distant bone or spur light up, use the Hook Tip to grapple onto it.

When you find a rune (joining ligaments to bone), you must ground pound
it ten times to destroy it—just like with the other colossus battles. When
destroyed, a nearby bone shatters allowing you to find the continuing route on
the beast.

After destroying the second rune (first two are on the top spine area) you can
work your way under the beast and find the third run inside the ribcage under
the monster.

After destroying the ribcage rune the monster throws you off, but you have an
opportunity to reattach to the beast by passing a single halo ring challenge.
Done correctly, Gabriel engages the Seraph Shoulders just in time to avoid
being eaten, then chain grips to a bone close to head.

When going for the last rune on the head, you must move back down the neck bones and drop from bone to bone along the lighter grey bone protrusion near the base of the neck. Slip around the end of the last pointy bone piece to get to the opposite side of the beast's head and move back up towards the head.

The fourth rune is found on top of the beast just below where its head connects to the neck. Beat this rune ten times to begin the final stage. You spot the final rune...in the boss's mouth.

Final Stage: The Fifth Rune

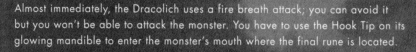

Once you find and destroy all the four runes on the boss's body, the final phase of the combat commences. The Dracolich stands before you hanging onto the edge of the platform, using its claws to grab the floating remains of the towers.

Almost immediately, the Dracolich uses a fire breath attack; you can avoid it but you won't be able to attack the monster. You have to use the Hook Tip on its glowing mandible to enter the monster's mouth where the final rune is located.

You are only able to hit the rune while the Dracolich opens its mouth to prepare its attack. If you fail to ground punch the rune in its mouth, no damage will be inflicted to the boss and you'll be ejected out of the mouth by way of a fire breath attack. If you do damage the rune, you are deposited out of his massive mouth back onto the battle platform. You only need to hit the rune twice. On the second hit, the Dracolich is utterly ruined.

CHAPTER XII

LEVEL ONE: FINAL FIGHT

And now the final battle is come. Marie is waiting for you, my friend. She knows what you have done. She knows everything. Marie has hoped all this time that you would save the world and here you are on the brink of it. You stand upon a knife edge. She has kept faith in you despite everything, now you must fulfill your destiny and the truth will out. I will help you, old friend. I will be with you in this your moment of victory!

Monsters

‡ Reaper   ‡ Satan

Unlockable Trial

‡ Finish the level and defeat Satan without being hit by any attacks with the opposite magic color

Satan is a powerful enemy. But you are the hero—you are given an endless supply of both Light and Shadow magic at your disposal during this fight.

Satan can use both types of magic, and you have to pay special attention to which type is he using. You have to attack him with the opposite type of magic to do any considerable damage. Matching opposite magics also replenish your health.

STAFF COLOR

The end of Satan's magic staff glows with a different color for each type of magic he's using. Watch for changes and try to react to them as fast as possible by changing to the opposite magic; even during combo attacks.

This mechanic also applies to you—Satan's attacks inflict much less damage if both characters are using the same type of magic, and vice versa.

During the combat, Satan also uses a trap type attack: he lays a series of moving magic symbols on the ground, colored red or blue with a random pattern. If you cross one of these symbols without the same type of magic (remember blue for Light Magic, and red for Shadow Magic), it entraps you until you switch to the correct color.

After you deal about a quarter of damage, Satan teleports to the opposite side of the platform and shields himself to recover some health. You must cross the layers of colored shields by using the same color of magic. If you fail to use the same color, the shields knock you back. When you reach Satan, press the Grab button to start the mini-game sequence.

The halo ring challenge doesn't appear until midway through the fight cinematic that is triggered by grabbing Satan when he is healing inside his multilayered shield. Press any button when the center halo glows and you punch Satan in midair.

Once you knock Satan up further into the air, another halo challenge appears when the two of you join up again. Hit it correctly and you send him to the ground. When he crawls out of the ground to fight again, a checkpoint is reached and stage two begins.

Stage Two

After the midair punching mini-game has past, the second phase starts. Satan adds a couple extra attacks to his repertoire, both of them are avoidable but only if you enable the same magic that Satan's attack uses.

When you've beat him down to but a fraction of his health, Satan repeats the same healing tactic as before, this time surrounding himself with moving magic shields. Pass through them quickly with the correct color magic engaged and perform a Grab on him to end the combat.

During the ending cinematic, there are a couple halo ring challenges. The first comes as you try to kick him back down into the ground. Fail and he regains health and you have to drain the second half of his health again to get back to this point.

The last halo challenge quickly follows the first. You must successfully pass the second halo challenge to hit him in the head with your Combat Cross.

Congratulations! You just have beat Castlevania: Lords of Shadow. Enjoy the awesome ending cinematic and the prize that follows the credits!

Trophies & Achievements

Achievement	Description	GS Awarded (XBOX 360)	Total Accumulated GS (XBOX 360)
Chapter I	Defeat the Ice Titan	10	10
Chapter II	Get the Dark Gauntlet	10	20
Chapter III	Acquire the power of the first Dark Lord	15	35
Chapter IV	Kill the Crow Witch	15	50
Chapter V	Gain access to the Vampire Castle	20	70
Chapter VI	Leave the Refectory with the Butcher's Key	20	90
Chapter VII	Survive the encounter with Laura	25	115
Chapter VIII	Acquire the power of the second Dark Lord	25	140
Chapter IX	Persuade Baba Yaga to open a portal to the Necromancer area	25	165
Chapter X	Vanquish the Gravedigger	30	195
Chapter XI	Acquire the power of the third Dark Lord	30	225
Chapter XII	Defeat Satan and save the world	35	260
Trials: Chapter I	Complete all the trials for Chapter I	25	285
Trials: Chapter II	Complete all the trials for Chapter II	25	310
Trials: Chapter III	Complete all the trials for Chapter III	25	335
Trials: Chapter IV	Complete all the trials for Chapter IV	25	360
Trials: Chapter V	Complete all the trials for Chapter V	25	385
Trials: Chapter VI	Complete all the trials for Chapter VI	25	410

Achievement	Description	GS Awarded (XBOX 360)	Total Accumulated GS (XBOX 360)
Trials: Chapter VII	Complete all the trials for Chapter VII	25	435
Trials: Chapter VIII	Complete all the trials for Chapter VIII	25	460
Trials: Chapter IX	Complete all the trials for Chapter IX	25	785
Trials: Chapter X	Complete all the trials for Chapter X	25	510
Trials: Chapter XI	Complete all the trials for Chapter XI	25	535
Trials: Chapter XII	Complete all the trials for Chapter XII	25	560
Master achiever	Complete all the trials	50	610
Dark collector	Gather all the 30 Shadow gems	20	630
Light collector	Gather all the 30 Light gems	20	650
Green collector	Gather all the 30 Life gems	20	670
Master jeweler	Gather all hidden magic gems	25	695
Master philanthropist	Buy all the extra artwork	20	715
Skirmish	Finish all levels in Esquire difficulty	15	730
Gest	Finish all levels in Warrior difficulty	20	750
Crusade	Finish all levels in Knight difficulty	30	780
Epic victory	Finish all levels in Paladin difficulty	40	820
Welcome to the Club	Buy a combo	15	835
Brawler	Buy 15 combos	20	855
Master fighter	Buy all combos	25	880
Experienced	Acquire 1000 experience points	10	890
Seasoned	Acquire 20000 experience points	15	905
Veteran	Acquire 100000 experience points	30	935
Master improver	Find all the secret Brotherhood arks	25	960
Eleventy party	Get 110% completion rate in all levels	40	1000

Extras

Unlockables

Difficulty Settings & 100% Level Completion

You can choose between one of the following four difficulty modes before playing each level: Esquire (easy), Warrior (normal), Knight (hard), Paladin (expert). You are free to change the difficulty level before starting each level. Paladin difficulty is not unlocked until you beat an entire Chapter while in Knight mode.

The level completion percentage is dependent on two things: the amount of collectible items (Magic Gems, Relics and Upgrades) you found in the level and the difficulty setting used while beating the level. Assuming you have collected all the items and upgrades in a level, the following chart will help you understand the level completion percentage per difficulty level chosen:

All Items Collected in this Mode:	Level Completion % Awarded
Esquire	60%
Warrior	68%
Knight	76%
Paladin	86%

You cannot achieve 100% in any mode until you have completed the unlockable Trial in that level.

Trials

Every level in every Chapter has a special challenge that's unlocked by completing the level *once* in any mode. The challenge is called a "Trial" and the details of the Trial appear on the Travel Book level completion stats page. Each level presents a unique challenge and once beat, you can achieve 100% completion for that stage—but only if you have chosen Knight or Paladin mode **and** have collected all the hidden collectibles and upgrades in that level. You cannot beat a Trial until it is unlocked, and this happens after completing the level once. So, even if you know the trial details beforehand and accomplish those tasks the first time through a level, you will not "accomplish" that trial. You must play the level a second time to do so.

The following chart illustrates your completion percentage per difficulty mode when you beat a Trial—while assuming you have collected all the hidden items and upgrades:

Beating the Trial in Mode:	Level Completion %
Esquire	84%
Warrior	92%
Knight	100%
Paladin	110%

To get 100% completion in a level, you must have collected all hidden items and upgrades while beating the challenge in Knight mode. If you do the same thing while in Paladin mode you reach 110% completion.

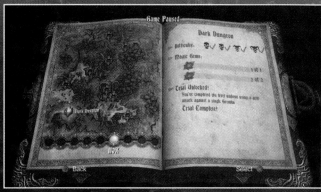

Artwork

About 80% of the artwork and concept art for the game must be purchased using experience points. The other 20% is unlocked through normal progression through the story. Artwork can be viewed in the Extras menu.

Snake Outfit

This is a customized outfit for Gabriel, resembling Solid Snake from Metal Gear Solid fame. This is available in the Extras menu once you have finished the game the first time. You can also choose to wear the bandana or not.

Combat Display

After you finish the first level in the game, the Combat Display option becomes available in the Extras menu. This allows you to turn on or off the following options:

Display Type	Description
Experience Gain	Shows orange EXPs floating from defeated enemies.
Enemies Health Bars	Displays a health bar below the enemy (this is the most helpful display option)
Gabriel's Health Bar	Displays a health bar below Gabriel (most redundant display; we don't recommend this one).
Gabriel's Combat Damage	Yellow damage points float up from enemies when you attack them. This helps you figure out which attacks are doing the most damage. When Dark Magic is enabled, you usually do more damage; these damage points are displayed in red.
Gabriel's Health Recovery	Green health points float up from Gabriel when healing at Health Font or using Light Magic.

Vampire Wargame

Vampire Wargame is unlocked and playable from the Extras menu when you beat the Vampire Wargame for the first time in Chapter VI, Castle Hall. If you chose to skip the challenge, the game will not be unlocked. You must beat the game without using the hint Scroll challenge skip. Once unlocked, the game becomes available Extras menu and you can select *One* or *Two* player.

Cheats

Cheats are unlocked in the Extras menu. The cheats allow you to turn the following functions on and off:

Cheat	Description
No Damage	Invincibility
All Relics	Discover all Relics
All Combos	Activates all Combos without purchasing
All Gems	Discover all Magic Gems
All Upgrades	Discover all Weapon & Relic Upgrades

To activate the cheat sub-menu where you can turn the above options on and off, you must input a special code on any of the level load screens (where the level introductory story is displayed and the "Press Start" message is located). Once the level loads and before you press "Start," input the following code using the D-pad and a couple buttons:

Cheating Deletes Your Save

Before entering the code, you must be aware of the consequence: cheats will deactivate your saved game and trophies (or Achievements).

Xbox 360
Up, Up, Down, Down, Left, Right, Left, Right, B, A

PS3
Up, Up, Down, Down, Left, Right, Left, Right, ◎, ✖

Castlevania
– Lords of Shadow –
Official Strategy Guide

DK/BradyGames, a division of Penguin Group (USA) Inc.
800 East 96th Street, 3rd Floor
Indianapolis, IN 46240

ISBN: 978-0-7440-1259-0

Printing Code: The rightmost double-digit number is the year of the book's printing; the rightmost single-digit number is the number of the book's printing. For example, 10-1 shows that the first printing of the book occurred in 2010.

13 12 11 10   4 3 2 1

Printed in the USA.

BradyGAMES Staff

Editor-In-Chief
H. Leigh Davis

Global Strategy Guide Publisher
Mike Degler

Digital and Trade Category Publisher
Brian Saliba

Credits

Senior Development Editor
Brian Shotton

Book Designer
Brent Gann

Production Designer
Tracy Wehmeyer